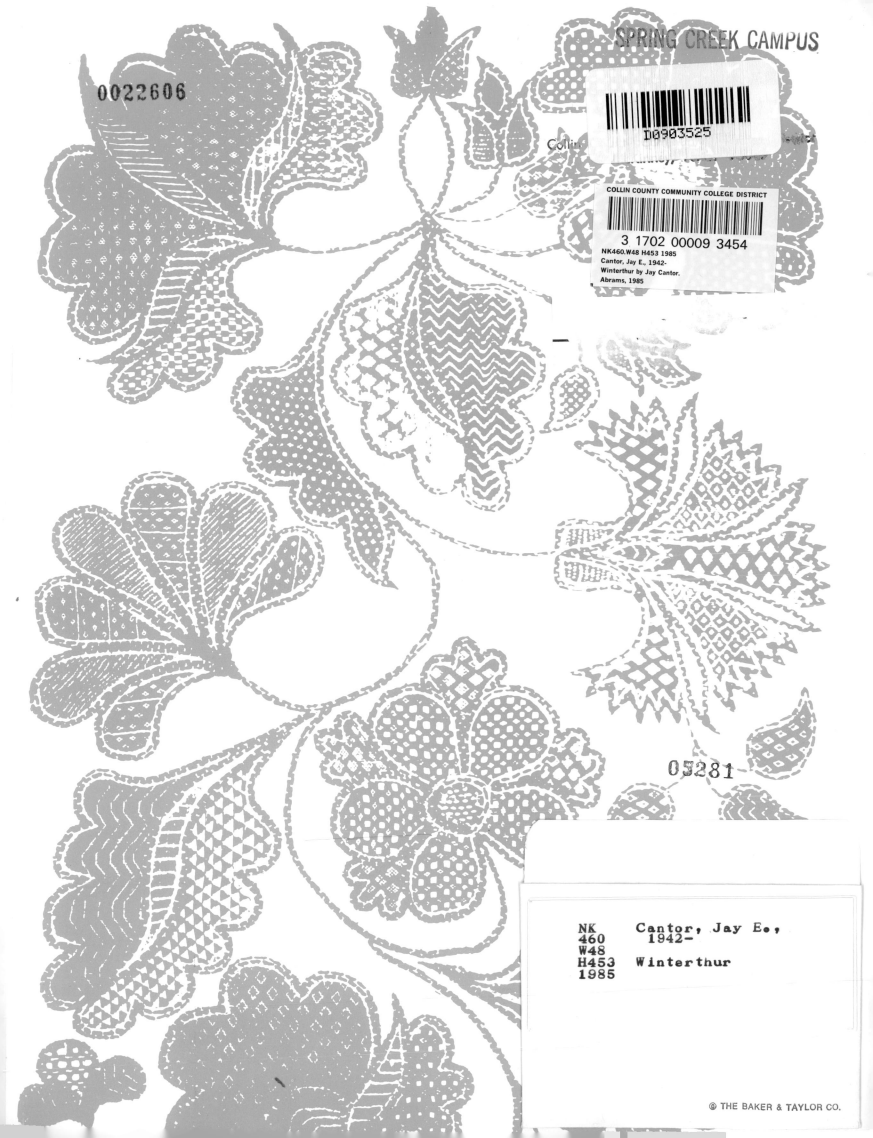

# WINTERTHUR

*Azalea Woods in spring*

*Port Royal Hall*

*Early nineteenth-century piano in the Federal Parlor*

*American looking glass in the Chinese taste in the Charleston Dining Room*

# WINTERTHUR

JAY E. CANTOR

ORIGINAL PHOTOGRAPHY BY LIZZIE HIMMEL

HARRY N. ABRAMS, INC., PUBLISHERS, NEW YORK

*Blue-and-white delft garniture on mantel in Bowers Parlor (previous page)*

*Curved chairback settee from New England, c. 1800. Mahogany, satinwood inlays, soft maple. Width: 84″*

Editor : Joan E. Fisher
Designer : Samuel N. Antupit

*Library of Congress Cataloging in Publication Data*

Cantor, Jay E., 1942–
Winterthur.

Includes index.
1. Henry Francis du Pont Winterthur Museum.
2. Decorative arts—Delaware—Wilmington.   I. Title.
NK460.W48H453   1985 745'.0974'07401511   85–3921
ISBN 0–8109–1785–8

*Carved eighteenth-century spoon rack from Middle Europe*

# CONTENTS

*Photographs by Lizzie Himmel copyright © 1985*
*Harry N. Abrams, Inc., and The Henry Francis*
*du Pont Winterthur Museum*
*Archival photographs copyright © 1985*
*The Henry Francis du Pont Winterthur Museum*
*Published in 1985 by Harry N. Abrams,*
*Incorporated, New York. All rights reserved.*
*No part of the contents of this book may*
*be reproduced without the written permission*
*of the publishers. Printed and bound in Japan*

*Detail of inlay from settee on page 10*

*Slip seat. American, 1730–70. Crewel yarns in tent stitch on fine linen, 14½ x 19⅛″*

# FOREWORDS

What do we, the children of Henry Francis du Pont, remember about Winterthur? First is the outdoors—the swaying watercress in Clenny Run Creek, mint, and forget-me-nots, bunches of which we picked for our mother's birthday every year. On the hills and meadows were dandelions, Queen Anne's lace, clover, and daisies that we often plucked and then left behind under our swings when the morning was over. A walk to the wild strawberry patch was a big event; the fruit was warm and delicious. So too was the fresh, foamy milk that the farmer gave us from one of the Holstein cows.

Outside the wrought-iron garden gates, next to a mossy path, was a goldfish pond in a grottolike spot. Inside the gates, at the end of the rose beds, was a formal pool where dragonflies swooped and frogs swam under the waterlilies. The pansies and columbines in the formal beds were to be looked at only, and the stands of foxgloves that grew as tall as two little girls were not to be used for hide and seek. The box bushes on the lawn and the big trees in the woods were better for games, anyway.

We are often asked what it was like to live in a museum. Of course, the museum grew slowly over the years. We became accustomed to piles of masonry, brick, dust, and the sounds and smells of building. For over a year while work was underway, our entire family moved into a small house at the foot of the hill near the creek. This was a happy time in our childhood, with our whole family sharing a tiny living room bright with chintz and firelight.

Though the Winterthur Museum did not officially open until 1951, we were surrounded by beautiful, breakable objects from babyhood, and

*Henry Francis du Pont, 1880– 1969. Creator of the Winterthur Museum and its collections, renowned gardener and pioneering cattle breeder, du Pont continued throughout his life to improve and enhance his surroundings, always making voluminous notes to aid this process*

17

we were taught to be very careful. Sitting on our beds was out of bounds once the bedspreads were on. We were often warned of the dangers of clumsiness when some grown-up guest knocked over and broke a valuable piece.

The presiding genius of our surroundings was our father, Henry Francis du Pont. Ably helped in every other aspect of life by our witty and talented mother, Ruth Wales du Pont, he alone formed the museum collection and spent hours of each day arranging it. The balance of his time was spent at work on the gardens, grounds, and farm. Harry du Pont had a wonderful eye for proportion and an extraordinary color sense, with the ability to remember and match colors long after seeing them. He made the rooms at Winterthur into works of art, using the furniture and objects of centuries past as his materials.

As children, we took artistic activities for granted and were more impressed by our father's tremendous energy. After a 6:00 a.m. breakfast of hot water and lemon juice, with the next meal not until 1:00 p.m., he could outlast and outwalk his daughters and everyone else. We smiled at each other when visitors sank into chairs, mopping their brows, at the end of a "little stroll to see the place."

Henry Francis du Pont loved Winterthur. It was his achievement, his birthplace, his home, and the place where he died. His enthusiasm for the house, the museum, and the land speaks to us still.

Ruth Ellen du Pont Lord
Pauline Louise du Pont Harrison

*Construction views, 1929. The extreme narrowness of the wing added between 1928 and 1931 was the result of the effort to fit this southern extension into a wooded hillside location and provide windows for all interior rooms*

18

When Jacqueline Bouvier Kennedy set about the task of redecorating and furnishing the White House in 1961, she appointed a distinguished committee to offer advice and assistance. There was one obvious choice to head the committee. The First Lady invited Henry Francis du Pont to serve as chairman of the Fine Arts Committee for the White House, and he promptly accepted the challenge. This particular form of recognition was only the most highly publicized of this complex man's many activities. He had by then already received three honorary doctoral degrees (from Yale, Williams, and the University of Delaware), plus numerous other awards and citations. The National Trust for Historic Preservation honored him with its Louise du Pont Crowninshield Award (named for his sister) in 1961, and the Garden Club of America presented him with its Medal of Honor in 1956. He was a member of the American Antiquarian Society, the Colonial Society of Massachusetts, the American Philosophical Society, and the Walpole Society. He served as a trustee of the Whitney Museum of American Art, the Philadelphia Museum of Art, and the New York Botanical Garden, to name just a few. Nathan Pusey of Harvard sent him a note of appreciation in 1966, recognizing his forty-two years as a member of the Overseers Committee to Visit the Arnold Arboretum. Thus, while he was creating a great museum, expanding and shaping a garden of immense beauty, and supervising a dairy farm that was a model of its kind, he still took the time to honor the concept of public service.

Winterthur also benefited from H. F. du Pont's sense of higher purpose. It is important to remember that no cultural institution arrives on the scene with an instant claim to a leadership role in national cultural affairs. Such a role must be earned through the demonstrated excellence of programs. When Winterthur opened its doors to the general public in

*Winterthur as it appeared in the 1930's, showing the earlier parts of the house to the left and the extended wing added by Henry Francis du Pont. The facade of the old house was redesigned to conform to the wing by its architect, Albert Ely Ives of Wilmington, Delaware*

1951, the founder and trustees could easily have decided that merely to display such a marvelous collection amid surroundings of such grandeur and beauty was accomplishment enough. Many house museums had done exactly that. Present at the museum's creation, however, were men and women with the vision and imagination to realize that here was an opportunity to do something significant. They realized that the collection should be studied in a serious way in order to provide intelligent interpretation. At the time, there were few professional scholars in American decorative arts, and no formal course of study existed in the field at an advanced level. The decision in 1952 to affiliate with the University of Delaware for the purpose of creating the Winterthur Program in Early American Culture, a two-year program of graduate study, was a crucial one for Winterthur. The graduate program assumed a major role in the development of the museum. The high level of interpretation, the research library, the publications program, the many conferences and seminars—indeed all of those things that have made Winterthur famous for its educational activities—largely came to pass because of the presence of the graduate program. The emphasis on graduate education continued with the founding in the 1970s of the Winterthur Program in the Conservation of Artistic and Historic Objects and, later in that decade, of the Ph.D. program in the history of American civilization. In recognition of all these programs and the accompanying research resources, the National Endowment for the Humanities in 1979 designated Winterthur a Center for Advanced Study.

H.F. du Pont enthusiastically supported the educational programs. He endowed chairs in the history, art history, and English departments at the University of Delaware. His endowment of the museum pays the salaries of curators, teaching associates, and others who serve the graduate programs. He provided the funds for building the Crowninshield Research Building at Winterthur to house expanded library facilities and conservation laboratories. He even treated the students to dinner and the theater once a year.

It is fitting, therefore, that Jay Cantor, a graduate of the Winterthur Program in Early American Culture (class of 1966), has written this fine account of the history and development of Winterthur. Mr. Cantor, who is vice-president, American paintings, at Christie, Manson & Woods in New York, worked extensively in the Winterthur archives, gathering information to tell the story of the great transformation of Winterthur under the leadership of H. F. du Pont. Mr. Cantor also interviewed family members, dealers, collectors, and employees who had worked with du Pont. His narrative is rich with anecdotes gleaned first-hand from those who had a part in the story. Lizzie Himmel's marvelous photographs provide visual counterpoint to the narrative. The book is a pleasure to read and a delight to behold. Its quality reflects the excellence that characterized Winterthur under Henry Francis du Pont and that I am charged with upholding as the recently appointed fifth director of Winterthur.

Thomas A. Graves, Jr.
*Director,* Winterthur Museum

21

# Winterthur Today: Museum and Gardens

WINTERTHUR. The name is foreign and often mispronounced. The place is lodged in the imagination like a legendary kingdom, remote and unlocatable. As with all romantic visions, the reality is more practical but is not complete without the dreamy dimensions from which myths are made.

The raw statistics of Winterthur are dazzling: over nine hundred acres of garden, meadow, and woodland, snatched from the ever-encroaching urban sprawl of the Atlantic corridor, shelter a mansion of nearly two hundred rooms and display areas. So many objects are there in those rooms that the staff can only roughly estimate their number—more than seventy thousand. The value of the objects is inestimable because of the sheer concentration of quality.

Nearly all of it belonged to one man: Henry Francis du Pont. His connoisseurship and zeal place him well above his contemporaries, and his reputation is still untarnished decades after his significant collecting activity ended. Du Pont engineered the assembly and installation of the collection in rooms with period woodwork from each of the original thirteen colonies. Winterthur itself had remained in the hands of the same family for nearly 150 years, making it virtually unique in a highly mobile American society. The collections span two centuries of creative productivity in American decorative arts, roughly 1640 to 1840.

Winterthur is situated along the northwestern edge of Delaware. The boundary separating northern Delaware from Pennsylvania is a piece of pure geometry, a perfect arc whose radius is centered in New Castle some thirteen miles away. It was along this border, nestled in the Bran-

*View along Clenny Run looking north toward the museum drive and one of the early farmsteads that have been incorporated into the Winterthur tract. Drifts of a single variety of daffodil in an irregular massing is a characteristic feature of du Pont's landscape approach*

dywine Valley, that the first du Ponts settled in 1802, two years after their landfall in America on the first day of the nineteenth century. The Brandywine Valley had long been attractive to settlers because of its fertility and proximity to ports in Philadelphia and Baltimore as well as its access to western hinterlands. The Brandywine River itself provided another desirable asset: water power. In its sixty-mile run through southeastern Pennsylvania and into northern Delaware, the Brandywine River gains enormous momentum that is greatly multiplied by a drop of 125 feet in its last five miles before emptying into the Delaware River at Wilmington. The combination of water power and port facilities at first spawned grain and textile mills and later encouraged the industry with which the region became endurably associated—black powder.

The French émigré Eleuthère Irénée du Pont quickly perceived the desirability of the Brandywine location for establishing a high-quality black powder manufactory much needed in America. The enterprise prospered and expanded, and the du Ponts settled comfortably into an enclave surrounding the mills to watch over production. The earliest family house, Eleutherian Mills, was constructed by the founder in 1802. It was occupied by the next du Pont generation until a massive explosion in 1890 so weakened the structure as to render it unsafe for habitation. The family conceived an enormous affection for their adopted soil and devoted considerable energy to its improvement. The landholdings were expanded and experimental farming and horticulture were avidly pursued. The land on which Winterthur sits today came into the family between 1810 and 1818; although much enlarged from the first farm tracts that were the foun-

*Winterthur today is composed of 963 acres of rolling landscape, including fields, meadows, and woodlands, and nearly two hundred acres of landscaped gardens. The irregularities of the natural terrain have been preserved and recall the century and a half of active agriculture on the site*

24

dation of the estate, the property resonates with echoes of its long history of family ownership.

When the visitor passes through the gates at Winterthur, there awaits more than just a vast collection of American decorative arts. The long drive curves down a hillside and past meadows and woodlands typical of an English landscape park. The hilly terrain provides a verdant backdrop to specimen plantings of shrubs and trees, which in springtime are covered with profuse blossoms, as much use has been made of flowering varieties. The plantings have been carefully positioned to create movement through the landscape while articulating vistas and providing splashes of color or lively contrasts of shape and form. The landscape has been consciously manipulated in a pictorial manner, and the first evidence of the controlling hand of Henry Francis du Pont becomes visible.

Winterthur assumed much of its current shape at the beginning of this century. The estate was melded out of a series of separate farms and lots; the reminders of those origins abound in the numerous farmhouses, barns, sheds, and service buildings that dot the landscape. The practical roots of this landscape are further emphasized throughout the property by a respect for the original contours of the land. Later, improvements were made to enhance the natural features so that a specific sense of place prevails. The landscape throughout much of its extent is more dignified than pretty, toughened by the practicalities of farm life and readily suggesting the familiar imagery of Andrew Wyeth, whose Chadds Ford, Pennsylvania, home is but a few miles away.

Farm activity is not as evident today as it would have been to a visitor during the first half of this century. The entry road to Winterthur is new and calculated to emphasize the pictorial qualities of the landscape. The road leads to a parking lot and a pavilion reception center, features created to serve the modern visitor. From the pavilion emanate the pathways and roads that introduce visitors to the gardens and lead them to the museum. The old entrance to Winterthur is one-half mile down the road at the present southeastern corner of the property.

The visitor to the estate when it was the du Pont home would have turned off the Kennett Pike at a modest gatehouse and passed beneath a covered entry, both structures clad in a gray-brown stucco. Along either side of the flat, curving, half-mile-long road leading to the house, meadows and pasture lands were actively employed, producing enviable crops and supporting a prize herd of Holstein-Friesian cattle. Some distance on the road entered a dense wood whose centuries-old trees were carefully guarded by the owners. Here and there a service road led to hillside barns, cutting gardens, a sawmill, or workers' tenant houses. Finally, the trees thinned in advance of a stream, Clenny Run, which meandered gently through a shallow valley. Across the stream on a woody hillside, the house loomed like a tawny leviathan in an emerald sea.

Despite its size, Winterthur sits comfortably within the landscape. It is overshadowed by lofty oaks and tulip poplars, and on two sides it faces woodland gardens that in springtime are set ablaze by a succession of floral displays ranging from the limpid yellows of naturalized narcissus, the burgundy pink of saucer magnolias, and the tissue mauves, pinks, lav-

enders, and vermilion of masses of mature Kurume azaleas. Crowned by steep orange-tiled roofs and set into the hillside so that several of its nine stories are subterranean, the immense dimensions of the house are obscured at first viewing. It is only after the visitor approaches closely that the scale becomes apparent. Aside from its monumentality, the facades of Winterthur suggest little of the interior riches. As if in keeping with the necessary functionalism of nearby farm buildings, the house is nearly bare of ornament. A parade of windows flanked by shutters alleviates the monotony, while the dominating roofs provide a controlling unity. This crown is studded with dormers whose profile is derived from examples taken from Port Royal, a house built on the edge of Philadelphia in 1762 and a building whose rich interior woodwork has been appropriated for some of the finest rooms at Winterthur. The doorway, set into an entrance pavilion and surmounted by a Palladian window, is in the center of the western facade of the house. It served as the principal entrance during Henry Francis du Pont's occupancy and is still used today.

After du Pont added a major extension in 1928, the building was a T-shape in plan and sited on a north-south axis. The T was slightly modified by a dogleg to the southwest containing a service wing. That has now been further extended and enlarged by additions for office and display areas, textile storage facilities, and a research building with art conservation and library facilities. Since its opening as a museum, Winterthur has had its entrance at the southernmost end, originally through the service wing and now through a vestibule designed for that purpose.

Whether one enters Winterthur through the old front door or through the new museum entrance, the effect of the place is the same. It

*Eleutherian Mills, the first du Pont residence on the Brandywine, overlooked the powder mill refinery. The building was restored by Louise Crowninshield, Henry Francis du Pont's sister, and is now open to the public. Drawn by the Baroness Hyde de Neuville in 1817 during one of her regular tours of the eastern United States*

is not through any logical sequence of rooms but rather through an accumulation of experience that the visitor comes to know and understand the collection and its purposes. The effects are achieved by the operation of a subtle and unobtrusive guiding hand. Winterthur is possessed of an overwhelming display of American and related decorative arts, exhibited without cases or barricades in room settings that not only evoke the spirit of the time from which the objects come, but also enable those objects to speak individually while contributing to an overall composition. In an effort to coerce the meanings out of objects, they have been combined for reasons beyond their function or visual harmony. The rooms at Winterthur can be understood as essays in style language in which regional preferences or thematic correspondences are presiding considerations.

The earliest rooms were designed in 1929 for the new wing built between 1928 and 1931. The rooms here served the dual function of display and daily use for the du Ponts. Formal parlors and dining rooms; smoking, dancing, and drawing rooms; and a host of bedrooms were seconded by a service wing and bath and dressing rooms. During the mid-1930s, the oldest portion of the house was reworked to incorporate more period interiors. Service spaces were commandeered and turned into display areas. The slow, inexorable transition from house to museum was begun. During this period, the domestic logic of the plan became obscured as new rooms were fitted into former service areas. One by one the Bowling Alley, Badminton Court, Squash Court, Ping-pong Room, and Billiard Room fell victim to a "higher calling." The resulting range of rooms and display areas has the distinction of being the most comprehensive group of period room settings in any American museum.

*Entrance portal of the 1928–31 wing at Winterthur was adapted from the Port Royal house built near Frankford, Pennsylvania*

Stereopticon views taken in May and July 1935.
The Port Royal Hall (above) led directly from
the front door to the upper garden terrace and
was furnished with some of the finest Chippendale furniture from the mid-Atlantic colonies.
The now vanished Dancing Room (opposite top)
with woodwork from Tappahannock, in Essex
County, Virginia, typified one of du Pont's earliest collecting enthusiasms—country furniture
and masses of hooked rugs. Du Pont's sitting room
(right), called the Lancaster Room from Belle
Isle, Litwalton, Lancaster County, Virginia, was
part of a suite that included the Cecil Bedroom
and several dressing rooms. These rooms served
as his office, and from here he directed the massive collecting campaign that brought more than
fifty thousand objects to Winterthur

These 1935 stereopticon views show the Winterthur rooms in their early maturity. Many served
the double purpose of display and daily use. Over
the ensuing fifteen years, some rooms were
altered as more appropriate furniture became
available. The seventeenth-century furniture in
the Wentworth Room (opposite top) (1673 with a
paneled wall dating from c. 1710) was relocated
in the Hart and Oyster Bay rooms after they
were installed in the renovated 1902 wing. The
painted panel on the back wall was reunited with
its original paneling when the Flock Room
replaced the Billiard Room (above) in the 1902
wing. In the Du Pont Dining Room (left), the
carved eagle over the fireplace was replaced by a
rare Gilbert Stuart Vaughan–type portrait of
Washington

31

When Henry Francis du Pont began collecting American objects in the early 1920s, native arts were still largely valued for their historic rather than their aesthetic attributes. They were more frequently encountered in historical societies than in art museums. But dramatic changes were afoot, and du Pont was a prime mover in the reevaluation of American arts on an aesthetic basis. It was during this same period that the American Wing opened at the Metropolitan Museum of Art, Henry Ford began the collections at Dearborn, Michigan, and created Greenfield Village, and John D. Rockefeller, Jr., provided the support for Colonial Williamsburg.

In all of these enterprises and a host of other institutions, the period room was adopted as the best way to exhibit American antiques. Henry Francis du Pont did not originate the idea of using period architecture as a sympathetic backdrop for American things. His contribution lies more in the quality of his eye and his judgment and in the consistently high levels he reached in acquisition and ensemble. Of his collecting activity du Pont wrote: "A philosophy of collecting is of necessity highly subjective. Each individual who collects anything of a serious nature thinks in increasingly creative terms, almost as if his growing collection were a kind of artistic medium. This is true, I think, because a foremost drive for the collector is a love of his materials. To him these are of such beauty or importance as to cause him to preserve them, by no means for himself alone, but in order to share his discoveries."

According to the first director of Winterthur Museum, Charles F. Montgomery, "For Henry Francis du Pont, the personification of the man of taste, the dream of beauty underlay the creation of the collections.... The beauty was various: handsome materials—rich in color, grain, or texture, and skillfully worked by that special magic of hand and eye called *craftsmanship*—were made part of a harmonious whole."

The rooms at Winterthur are not obviously decorated. Nourished as we are by decorating, design, and lifestyle magazines that provide an inexhaustible anthology of decorating solutions, it is easy to forget how radical it was for someone of wealth and culture to devote himself to colonial antiques in the heyday of collecting French and English furniture.

But Henry Francis du Pont was in the advanced legion of connoisseurs in the field who turned connoisseurship into a tool of scholarship and display into high art. He began as a collector and through that activity became an authority. Through his installations, du Pont also became an active interpreter of the objects he collected and referred to them as "evidences of early life in America." Evidences which, according to Montgomery, tell us how our forebears "lived in their homes and communities, revealing aspects of their technology, trade, internal relations, social relationships, standards of living, folk heroes, tastes, values, and symbols."

What impresses the visitor to Winterthur beyond the quality of the collections is the rightness of it all. A typical room at Winterthur reveals itself as a series of layers. The rooms, like the man who created them, are a curious combination of discipline and personality. In an oft-quoted statement, du Pont revealed his dominating aesthetic principle: "It is one of my first principles that if you go into a room, any room, and right away

Maple furniture, often the product of rural cabinet shops, reflects the craftsman's response to the
wood's flamboyant grain and rich honey color. In
the Maple–Port Royal Hall, the curves of a mid-
eighteenth-century Pennsylvania bookstand mirror the scroll arms of a New England easy chair.
The Rhode Island candlestand is embellished
with a complicated pattern of turnings

Coordination between furniture and decorative
objects in a room is the hallmark of Henry Francis du Pont's display technique. The relationships
are both visual and historical. In the Montmorenci Stair Hall, a large punch bowl (above) of
Chinese export porcelain made for John Seawell
of Gloucester County, Virginia, is decorated with
four vignettes relating to the hunt. It provides a
dramatic accent in the sparsely furnished hall.
By contrast, the quantity of objects in the Franklin Room (opposite) is brought into harmony by
controlled positioning in the room. Many objects
stress the importance of national heroes in the
early federal period. The waxwork memorial to
George Washington on the far wall was made
for the American market by John Christian
Rauschner after Washington's death in 1799. The
English earthenware statuette of Benjamin
Franklin, on the table below, is carefully but mis-
takenly labeled Washington. A bust portrait of
Franklin embellishes the mantel

see something, then you realize that it shouldn't be in the room." Although not radical, the statement is revealing. Henry Francis du Pont was born in the waning years of the reign of Queen Victoria and grew up in a period when furniture announced its presence in a room with a clarion voice. Not surprisingly, subsequent generations sought a quieter approach to domestic convenience, buttressed by the pleadings of a body of reformers whose number included such unlikely companions as William Morris, John Ruskin, Gustav Stickley, Edith Wharton, and Elsie de Wolfe. While each espoused a different doctrine of true taste, they all had as their singular goal the banishment of high Victorian extravagance in favor of more demure furnishings. The taste for early American furniture grew to a certain extent out of that spirit of reform.

Henry Francis du Pont strove for classic principles: harmony, balance, order, and symmetry. There is in this structure a clear musical analogue, and one contemporary noted: "Harry du Pont is like a conductor of music. He may not know how to play each and every instrument, but he knows how to blend them together exquisitely." Yet in creating a well-tempered environment, there was also a renegade spirit, a taste for opposing musical modes. In his subtle and evocative moods, he was pure Debussy—but he also had his Wagnerian side, showing a predilection for full symphonic effects and massive scale (his favorite opera was *Die Walküre*).

If there was something of the musician in du Pont's approach, there was also a strong painterly instinct, derived in part from a sixty-year involvement in the creation of the gardens at Winterthur. He favored subtle color harmonies against which he isolated strong accents to create dra-

A Pennsylvania box of 1730–1800 and a walnut
chest attributed to Chester County, Pennsylvania,
1750–1800, feature a regional characteristic in
the vine-and-berry pattern of inlay. Such inlays
were not common in fashionable furniture of the
period, which was made of richly grained, elaborately carved mahogany. This inlay reflects a vernacular tradition of surface ornamentation but is
the product of sophisticated craft technique

The highly carved mantel in the Blackwell Parlor,
from the 1764 Blackwell house in Philadelphia,
features scenes from the fables of Aesop and La
Fontaine with carved flowers, garlands, and
scrollwork. Lavish carving of the pierced splat
and seat rail of the Philadelphia mahogany side
chair distinguish it and related examples as the
finest work produced by the city's ablest craftsmen. Together the architecture and furniture of
this room demonstrate the sophistication
achieved by the mid-eighteenth century in William Penn's Greene Country Town, which had
grown to be the largest city in Britain's American colonies

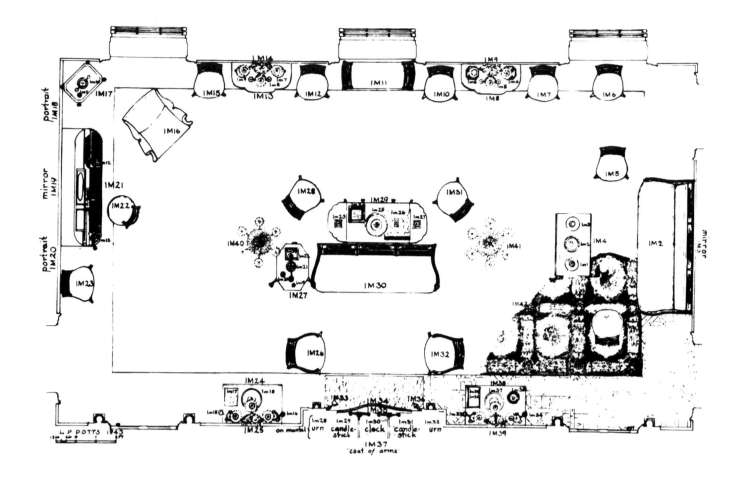

matic impact. He was attached to the faded tones of old paint in woodwork and labored with his painter to reproduce the effect by devising
color washes which would blend the newer moldings and woodwork that
was necessitated when old rooms were integrated into the uncompromising new structure. Against such tones the bold voice of major pieces of
furniture or the lush profusion of drapery would often resonate.

John Sweeney, former curator of Winterthur, has effectively described du Pont's attitude toward subtle colors in an episode involving re-
production fabric: "When the fragility of pale-blue lampas used on the
chairs in the Phyfe Room reached the point where the material had to be
replaced, the silk was reproduced in France on special order. The reproduced material, accurate in design and weave, was much stronger in color
based on chemical analysis of the original threads. It did not appeal to Mr.
du Pont; he permitted only the most threadbare chairs to be re-covered
and always referred [to] those retaining the antique upholstery as 'our
good chairs.'"

Over the years, documentation and authenticity became of increasing concern, but du Pont also had a passion for detail that although not
always recognized is nonetheless felt. In a characteristic vein, du Pont
wrote a friend in 1933: "After looking at my dining room summer curtains for two summers, I suddenly decided the other day that I could not
bear to see the modern fringe on them another minute. The curtains, by
the way, are that purple and white toile de jouy. As luck would have it, I
found in the storeroom a tremendous lot of antique braid which Mrs. Benkard got for me once in Savannah, and found it just matches the summer

38

Phyfe Room and plan. Woodwork from Moses Rogers house, built 1794, renovated c. 1806, 7 State Street, New York City. The drawing by Leslie Potts shows the balanced arrangement of furniture favored by du Pont. The drawing is typical of the plans made to document each room after the furnishing was completed. Such plans would also document the seasonal changes made in many rooms and would indicate changes of rugs, window hangings, and furniture coverings. Among the furniture by Duncan Phyfe in this room are chairs from a set made for William Bayard, who lived at 6 State Street, adjoining Moses Rogers. The elaborate gilt and painted chimney glass, c. 1805, was originally owned by Governor Joseph C. Yates of Albany and was made either there or in New York City

rug and gives such a pep to the curtains as you would not believe. I am now hoping that I may be able to find some day something to do the same to the reception room [Port Royal Parlor] curtains below the dining room. It is absurd, but really modern fringe kills every kind of antique material. There is a certain queer, standing-out harsh quality about it which is unbelievably bad." After discussing a similar change intended in another room, he indicated exactly how far his collecting tentacles had reached: "Just after ordering this, I received a letter from a woman in Italy offering me a sample of pink and blue fringe which is just the thing for the bedspread in that same room. So I really have had quite a successful time in the fringe world this summer."

Du Pont once remarked, "It has taken all these years to get all the correct furniture we needed, and needless to say every time a paneled room or mantelpiece was installed, I moved to this room the furniture that suited it." Although he spoke in terms of furniture, du Pont's collecting enthusiasms were wide ranging. In order to give "pep" to his rooms, he amassed significant quantities of lighting fixtures and devices, pottery and glass, English delft and Chinese export porcelain, fabrics from most continental countries and England dating after 1640, wallpaper and oriental rugs, silver, pewter, and other metalwork. In contrast to these largely high-style products, he also collected extensively in country arts and amassed a superb collection of Pennsylvania German art and artifacts. Because he was collecting at a time when little documentary research was available, he followed period conceptions of what was appropriate for American interiors. While some of the objects are overly

The rooms at Winterthur abound in evidences of early life in America. The five-legged New York card table in the Bertrand Room (top) is set with appropriate gaming paraphernalia, including cards, counters, and game box with pegs for scoring. The brass candlesticks are reminders of the dependence on localized illumination for most indoor activities. The side chairs, with their elaborate tassel and ruffle splats, belonged to Stephen Van Rensselaer, last patroon of the Manor at Albany. The brightly decorated Pennsylvania

German blanket chest (above left) from Berks County is filled with typical household textiles and retains its Fraktur, illuminating the story of Adam and Eve through painted designs and printed text. It is attributed to Frederick Speyer. Closets were not features of Pennsylvania German households. Clothes were folded or hung on pegs in the large traditional wardrobes, or shonks. The clothes tree in the Pennsylvania German bedroom (above) is a further reminder of that tradition

Prints of William Hogarth's engraved depiction
of John Wilkes, Esq., a popular English defender
of American liberties, were issued on May 16,
1763. The depiction reappeared on this Chinese
export porcelain bowl (above) in about 1775. The
bowl was probably ordered by an ardent patriot or
supporter of the American cause. Punches laced
with spirits were frequently served in the eighteenth century. The Massachusetts maple chair,
1725–75, and New England octagonal-top table,
also of maple, 1725–50, are typical of the plainer,
less expensive sort of furniture that might have
been found in a tavern

elaborate and there is a greater profusion of them in the rooms than would have logically existed, American arts were so little valued at the time that this overstatement was necessary to make the point.

Du Pont not only had a broad interest in corollary material that was carefully examined for quality of design and execution but he also paid attention to the smallest detail of ornament. The engraving on a drawer pull, the matching of veneers, the relationship of carving and ornament on two seemingly disparate objects were all within his focus. And it is often such lovingly observed details that provide the animating spirit of a room. Sequestered in table tops or hidden in closets and corners are objects that document the living conditions and social attitudes of the American past.

From musical instruments to playing cards, nursing bottles in glass and pewter to mourning rings of silver and gold, from swords and dueling pistols to the equally deadly instrument of political cartoons, from the most common woodenware to the highest sophistication in carving on Philadelphia Chippendale furniture, from everyday blankets and towels to the fanciful elaborations of crewelwork bedhangings, from miniature furniture and toys to the shop and tools of a rural cabinetmaking family in Long Island, Winterthur is a collection of collections. Within each style period, the full implications of form and ornament are explored. Even the lowly fireplace opens out into a room a veritable cornucopia spewing an abundant harvest. Mantel shelves are ornamented with delft, Staffordshire, export porcelain, earthenware, carved garnitures, clocks, and candlesticks. The fireplace tools, bellows, kettles on stands, trammels and

Innovations in lighting and heating, including style changes and functional improvements, are illustrated throughout the collections. In the Billiard Room, a branched candelabrum on the mantel (opposite) is made of plated copper, an improvement in Sheffield plate that made mass production easier. The mantelpiece has cast plaster composition ornaments made by Zane and Chapman in Philadelphia, and it bears their label. In the Kershner Parlor, a Pennsylvania copper tea kettle sits on a five-plate iron stove (above) cast at the Mary Ann Furnace in Manheim, Lancaster County, Pennsylvania, in 1766. The stove is set into the wall and opens into the fireplace in the adjacent room where it can be fed with fuel directly

Watch holder, American, 1800–1850. Painted
tulipwood. Height: 14⅝". Popular in mid-eighteenth-century America, watch holders positioned timepieces upright to ensure that they
would continue to work. Watch mechanisms were
so delicate that they would often stop if laid
down

peels, warming pans, andirons and firedogs, and fenders and firebacks suggest the development of baroque, rococo, or neoclassical forms that are replicated at a larger scale by other objects in a particular setting. Everything in these rooms was carefully scrutinized, fiddled with, weighed, and considered for its relationship to the whole. Once the exact position was determined, the spot was marked to ensure that the precise effect would be perpetuated.

A walk through the galleries of many museums makes it painfully clear how lifeless a period room can be. To inject vitality that suggests function and use and brings the visitor into close contact with the object, thereby forming or possibly reforming his vision, requires an inspired hand. Given the raw material of individual rooms, du Pont then organized a relationship of rooms that retell the chronicle of American design from the mid-seventeenth to the mid-nineteenth century.

Winterthur has been open to the public for more than three decades; during that time research in the field of American decorative arts has expanded and intensified. The resulting knowledge has not only confirmed much of what collectors of Henry Francis du Pont's generation knew by intuition or learned by a hands-on approach but it also has greatly expanded our understanding of how the colonial and early federal periods looked and felt and behaved. Where possible, this new information is reflected in the rooms at Winterthur, enlarging the visitor's understanding of period attitudes. Winterthur today represents the creative energies of America's founding populations and the resourcefulness of Henry Francis du Pont in amassing this vast collection. It reveals a hundred-year chronicle of changing attitudes toward the history of American decorative arts and their effective interpretation.

The second great collection at Winterthur is the gardens. A reciprocal relationship between house and grounds was planned and nurtured. The parallels between house and garden developments are numerous. As the architecture of the rooms at Winterthur influenced the organization of the furnishings, so the varied topography of the natural landscape was the dominating force in the organization and arrangement of the gardens. Henry Francis du Pont was exhaustive in his studies of plant varieties and was omnivorous in his acquisition of specimens for consideration. New specimens were tested for several years to observe their color, growth habits, and suitability to the Delaware environment. Careful consideration of the ultimate size and shape of a plant was given before a specimen was introduced into the garden; offenders in the overall harmonic scheme were removed.

In the gardens, as in the house, the approach was visual. Henry du Pont was a horticultural gardener, not a botanical one. Greenhouses were not display areas but were the laboratories for developing specimens from cuttings, experimenting with hybrids, and developing the massive volume of annuals required to fill in after early bulb plantings had gone by. Even in the depths of winter the house was alive with floral displays. During the blooming seasons, the quantities of flowers in the house were overwhelming, with as many as ten arrangements in each public room. In choosing flowers for the house, bold profusion rather than mixed arrangements dominated. Massive punch bowls and soup tureens were filled with flowers of one variety and color, with the same arrangement repeated throughout a particular room. In the dining room, table services, place mats, and accessories were all conditioned by the color range available for table-top arrangements. A conservatory attached to the northern side of the house contained displays orchestrated by du Pont with forced flowers and included plants and trees arranged according to seasonal celebrations or a particularly exciting discovery made in the greenhouse. Although the conservatory and flower arrangements in the house today only hint at their former splendor, the gardens themselves still provide a perfect index of the horticultural skills that won for du Pont an enduring reputation as one of the country's great gardeners.

The natural feeling of Winterthur's landscape is the product of carefully considered planning, and a leisurely stroll through any portion of the nearly two hundred landscaped acres reveals an endless array of trees, shrubs, and native and exotic flowers. Hundreds of thousands of bulbs have been naturalized at Winterthur over the decades and some of the special delights of springtime are the extraordinary drifts of narcissus splashed over various hillside locations. In fact, it is during the spring that Winterthur assumes its most extraordinary landscape personality.

Spring begins early, with Chinese witch hazels in full bloom by early March, followed later in the month by yellow-flowered cornel dogwoods and Korean forsythia. Thousands of snowdrops and snowflakes bloom white in the woodlands, along with lavender crocuses and the yellow adonis and winter aconite. More bulbs—squills, glory-of-the-snow, daffodils—come into bloom so that by April first the floors of the woodland are carpeted in many colors. Early rhododendrons, forsythias, cherries, and magnolias are flowering by mid-April.

Later in April, lilacs, flowering quinces, spireas, viburnums, and cherry, princess, and crabapple trees color the gardens until the first Kurume azaleas and Dexter hybrid rhododendrons usher in the month of May. The vanishing bulb flowers give way to myriad wildflowers—spring beauties, violets, trout lilies, trilliums, phloxes, and Virginia bluebells. Exbury azaleas are at their best during May, as are native azaleas, some of which bloom into summer. Hybrid herbaceous and tree peonies and candelabra primulas are also in flower during May and extend well into June.

The heat and humidity of a Delaware summer are kind to trees, shrubs, and meadows but not to tender blossoms. In the summer, there is a final wave of color: late lilacs, mountain laurels, deutzias, weigelas, and mock oranges are in full bloom on the first of June. During early June the Satsuki azaleas open their enormous flowers, while native azaleas continue the show—flame azaleas in early June, sweet and Cumberland azaleas at mid-month, and plum-leaf azaleas extending into July.

Woodland bulbs and wildflowers, shaded now by a thick canopy of leaves, have finished blooming, but colorful flowers of meadow and field appear. The woodland paths provide a cool and welcome relief to the steamy laziness of a summer day. The pungent odor of box fills the air, and hostas, hydrangeas, albizzias, vitex, althea, and stewartias lend a tropical density to the plantings.

The blaze of autumn color is made especially spectacular by the

46

*Chinese Parlor, 1935 stereopticon. This room was created out of two rooms on the main floor of the original 1839 Winterthur house. It was conceived as a display area for Chippendale furniture and as an area in which to show the exotic sources of its design and ornament, such as the gothic and Chinese detailing on chair splats, table fretwork, and stretchers. The room is a connecting link between the 1902 wing to the north and the 1928–31 southern wing. The room was the precise height of the wallpaper but when an interior wall was removed it became necessary to put a steel beam in the ceiling to support fireplaces in the upper story. The walls then had to be coved to adjust to the lowered ceiling height to provide sufficient space for the paper*

*Port Royal Parlor, May 1935 stereopticon. This grand reception room, the Chinese Parlor, and other public rooms were kept filled with flowers from the greenhouses and cutting gardens. Du Pont preferred lush arrangements of a single variety in large punch bowls and tureens. He positioned as many as a dozen arrangements in a single room and carefully coordinated them with the color of the textiles and woodwork*

scale of the huge ancient trees, and as the land turns to umber and the furrows of the plowed fields give a corduroy blanket to the rolling hills, berried shrubs come into their own, a last reminder of the flowers of springtime.

There are flowers during the fall also. In September, Oak Hill is covered with the lavender cups of colchicums. Early in October, the fall sternbergia with cups of gold join them, and a bit later, blue and white autumn crocuses appear. In the woodlands, blue and white wood asters bloom, while meadows are purple and gold with tall goldenrods and New England asters.

During the winter, when the trees are bared of their foliage, their amazing size becomes evident. Seen in clusters against snow-mantled fields and the thick gray of a winter sky, the trees' silhouettes suggest the promise of nature in its dormancy. On a hillside to the east of the house, a tall stand of mature conifers looks remarkably defiant against the blanched terrain. This mature Pinetum containing more than fifty species of evergreens was begun seventy years ago by Henry Algernon du Pont, Henry Francis's father, and suggests that he, like his son, was laying foundations for the future and looking well down the road toward some moment when the product of his energy and activities would be seen and used by other generations.

*The gardens at Winterthur are largely natural-
ized plantings. Henry Francis du Pont worked on
the grounds for more than sixty-five years, and
the mature plants, shrubs, and trees still reflect the
pictorial sequences of blooming time and color
relationships he strove for. The color relationship
among the spring starflower, flowering crabapples,
and cherry in the Sundial Garden (preceding
page) reveals the importance of spatial positioning in du Pont's schemes. The northern facade of
the museum (top) is dominated by a conservatory
added when du Pont altered his father's 1902
wing. The earlier landscape experiments carried*

*out by du Pont after he returned to Winterthur
from college in 1903 involved massive plantings of
bulbs for naturalizing in the woods opposite this
northern front. Other areas of naturalized bulbs
include daffodil beds along the present front
drive (above right) seen in this view looking toward the nursery area, where new introductions
were tested for their color, growth habits, and
adaptability to the Delaware climate. Such exotic
rarities as the Sawara cypress (above left) suggest the feverish activity in the expansion of
American horticultural practice that began in
the later nineteenth century*

The woods cover large portions of Winterthur's more than nine hundred acres and in spring are alive with flowering dogwood (top), which provide a lacy skirt for centuries-old trees. On the woodland floor periwinkle carpets the ground, creating a tapestry backdrop for broad-leafed trillium (left). Boldly scaled saucer magnolias in Magnolia Bend (above), at the terminus of the March Walk, provide the first evidence of the dense colors that animate the woods when the mature Kurume azaleas blossom later in May (following pages)

Winterthur's plantings embrace a variety of landscapes and visual effects. Low plantings such as Spanish bluebells (top) line paths along the route to the Azalea Woods and provide a color co-ordinate to Kurume azaleas (above). Then, enjoyment of the outdoors was extended by tennis courts and a ten-hole golf course (right), whose fairways were planted with naturalized daffodils. During the sporting season, players were not allowed to retrieve balls that landed in the daffodils

Winterthur's gardens were built around the natural conformation of the land. The rolling hillsides of the fertile Brandywine Valley provided a verdant backdrop for specimen plantings, and there were fields and meadows for the cultivation and grazing of Winterthur's prize herd of Holstein-Friesian cattle. The bucolic landscape still recalls English parklands. The railroad station, now a residence, adds to the picturesque setting. The dense woodlands are alive with a changing display of color produced by the Kurume azaleas and rhododendrons that were established after a chestnut blight created gaps in the ancient woods around the house. The Pinetum (overleaf), developed early in the century by Henry Francis du Pont's father, Henry Algernon, now boasts more than fifty varieties of mature conifers. Henry Francis was especially fond of the effect of azaleas against the dark trunks of woodland trees or against the blue-green needles of conifers. A passionate record keeper, he energetically kept track of the blossoming sequence of his plantings to improve their positioning and extend their visual impact

55

The painterly approach to garden organization was first developed in England and was eagerly adopted by Henry Francis du Pont at Winterthur. The most interesting facade of the wing he added to Winterthur was the east side (overleaf), which faced the terraced gardens and the surrounding woods where he carried out his naturalizing experiments. The building front became a feature in his garden and in landscape vistas. Two pairs of monumental stairs flowed down from an upper terrace to the swimming pool (above right) immediately to the east and on the south side to the now vanished rose and other terrace gardens. Dense or dramatic plantings of a single variety, such as the Chinese snowball viburnum bordering the Quince Walk (top) and the Peony Garden (above left) with its Summer House from the nineteenth-century Wilmington estate Latimeria, are typical of the way du Pont organized his landscape compositions. The Peony Garden replaced the iris beds after the latter were plagued by disease and pests. Although he was intrigued by specimen plants, he did not attempt an encyclopedic approach but a more purely visual one

Cut flowers for Winterthur's rooms came from specialized cutting gardens. The four walk-in refrigerators on the estate preserved fresh blossoms for the lavish interior arrangements that perfumed the entire house. Frequently, an especially beautiful individual flower would be cut and placed in its own container (occasionally a jelly glass) on a table top. After Winterthur was opened to the public, du Pont extended the plantings in the area of Oak Hill (above right) and elsewhere to lengthen the blooming season for visitors

The plantings near the house (preceding pages and top) show a rapid change of color and variety. The vista through the Peony Garden presents striking contrasts of the beautybush and a drift of deep red azaleas. Two steps beyond, the palette changes and Saunder's hybrid tree peony is seen against the mauve azaleas complemented by a

Japanese maple with its characteristic purple foliage. Although Henry Francis du Pont was not known as an innovative plant hybridizer, he is memorialized in Rhododendron mucronatum, or Magnificum Winterthur, a species developed by du Pont, seen under native beech trees along the Garden Lane near Oak Hill (above left). Other hybrid rhododendrons take a prominent place in the woods and along the new paths established since the museum opened

*Although du Pont especially liked purples and mauves, white-flowered plants found an important place in the garden and continued the theme first established by the flowering dogwoods in early spring. The white Kurume azaleas occupy a central position in the Azalea Woods (top) and mediate between the strong drifts of other colors. The mossy banks of Quarry Creek (above) provide the ideal environment for a glade densely planted with Asiatic candelabra primroses. Fern walks and grottoes were a part of the landscape plans developed by du Pont and his landscape architect, Marian Cruger Coffin, who was especially important in creating the planting scheme around the terrace gardens*

63

# EVOLUTION OF A COUNTRY PLACE

H enry Francis du Pont was born at Winterthur, Delaware, on May 27, 1889. He and his sister Louise du Pont Crowninshield were the only surviving children of seven born to Colonel Henry Algernon and Pauline Foster du Pont. In later years, Henry Francis du Pont was to state: "I was born at Winterthur and I have always loved everything connected with it." Winterthur had been his parents' home since 1875, when they gained title to the property on the death of the colonel's father, Henry, in 1889. Henry had been the president of the Du Pont Company for forty-nine years, the longest tenure of any president, and had been responsible for significant expansion of the company and a corresponding increase in the company's market share largely through the operation of a black powder trust.

*The Pinetum, with its massive, ancient trees, is the natural equivalent of the Winterthur house*

The initial acreage constituting the Winterthur tract had been acquired by the company's founder, Eleuthère Irénée du Pont, between 1810 and 1818. He had greatly enlarged the family's landholdings along the Brandywine River as the company grew and prospered. Wars and westward expansion had required black powder, and du Pont's energy and enthusiasm paid considerable dividends. Yet despite prosperity, the family was firmly rooted in close proximity to the flourishing powder mills. The business remained a tightly controlled partnership throughout the nineteenth century, and the family formed itself into an equally tightly knit social unit. They seemed content to live on the edge of the noisy, foul-smelling, and dangerous mills, and they expended much energy in improving their houses and gardens.

Gardening was, in fact, a special preoccupation of the family fos-

tered by Eleuthère's training and lifelong interest in botany. He had established a large garden at his home, Eleutherian Mills, soon after its construction and carried on an active correspondence on botanical issues, engaging in wide-ranging exchanges of plant material. This botanical and horticultural interest descended through succeeding generations of the family. There was, according to Norman Wilkinson, the chronicler of Eleuthère's botanical interest, "a steady exchange of things from one another's gardens and greenhouses. Seeds were shared and cuttings from new specimens passed around. A particularly beautiful flower or unusual shrub would be called to the attention of the entire family. Birthdays, anniversaries, the marriages of sons and daughters and of nephews and nieces, moves to a new home, the arrival of babies, and the frequent visits of relatives and close friends were all celebrated by gifts of flowers, flowering shrubs and ornamentals, and sometimes by the giving of young trees."

The Winterthur property was a part of the acreage Eleuthère devoted to experimental farming and animal husbandry. It was inherited by his heirs and sold by them to James Antoine Bidermann, the husband of Eleuthère's daughter Evelina. Bidermann had come to America in 1814 as a representative of the European investors in the du Pont enterprise to review the company's operations. He remained in Delaware, joining the company and ultimately becoming Eleuthère's sole partner. He had married Evelina the year after his arrival and joined other family members in residing in the family compound, but after his retirement from active participation in the company he decided to build a country seat on the 445-acre parcel he had acquired in 1837. The construction of the first Bi-

dermann house was begun in 1839 and by 1842 it was known as Winterthur, named for Bidermann's ancestral home in Switzerland. Designs had actually been drawn for Bidermann by N. Vergnaud in Paris but the house as erected had a very American look. A squat, flat-roofed Greek revival structure of stucco-covered stone, its principal architectural elaborations were a columnar portico on the north facade and a conservatory porch on the opposite front. The house was positioned on a rise above a shallow valley. It was placed in a woody setting surrounded by evergreen, oak, beech, hickory, and tulip trees. From its elevated position, one could survey Clenny Run, which wound through the valley floor before joining the Brandywine River a mile and a half away. From here Bidermann also surveyed the vestiges of Eleuthère's experimental farm and devised schemes to continue progressive work in scientific farming, while improving the property with gardens and other amenities appropriate to a country seat of landed gentry. Among his improvements were gatehouse and gatekeepers' dwelling, carriage house, and stables. He retained an early farmhouse on the property and installed machinery, including a waterwheel to feed a reservoir and a bathhouse. In addition to orchards and cutting gardens, the property boasted a sunken garden, a small greenhouse, and a dairy.

On Bidermann's death in 1866 the house passed to his only son who resided in France and was actively pursuing a career in railroad engineering. Not wishing to leave France, Irénée Bidermann was happy to accept his uncle's purchase offer for the property, an offer that would guarantee that the property remained in family hands. Henry du Pont

*Winterthur from the northeast (opposite); photograph dated 1883. View from the southeast (above left) looking across Clenny Run shows the house in its woodland setting. Winterthur was occupied by Henry Algernon du Pont (above) and his family after his marriage in 1874*

67

bought the property for his son Henry Algernon, a West Point graduate and career officer who had seen active service in the Civil War. When Colonel Henry Algernon du Pont announced his engagement to Pauline Foster in 1874, work began on renovating the Winterthur house and clearing the overgrowth that a few years of tenant farming and general neglect had created.

Before the couple departed on their European honeymoon, they went on an inspection tour of the property with the colonel's mother, who reported afterward: "We all went up to Winterthur today to see it and to show Pauline the spring and ferns and all the lovely wood paths around the house. She seems delighted with it & is a perfect sunbeam." By the end of the summer, progress had been made in clearing out the matted roots and briars and Mrs. du Pont happily informed the newlyweds: "You will have a supply of ordinary winter vegetables. The strawberry beds have just been planted...and the ground is ready for raspberries this fall as soon as the leaves drop from the plants. The asparagus bed is in good condition, planted last spring. Also some dwarf fruit trees & we have good grape vines well started ready for this fall....The old forcing house in the garden is to be put in order so that Pauline may have some flowers this winter." Winterthur was ready for its most important period of growth and development. The amenities of a "country place" were well established and with the architectural embellishments and increase in acreage that would come in the next decades, Winterthur was advancing toward its modern dimensions.

68 The house was enlarged several times during Colonel du Pont's oc-

cupancy. In 1884, the flat roof was raised, giving it a steep pitch. Verticality was further emphasized by fanciful dormers and tall brick chimneys. This expansion provided much-needed room for the enlarged family and lent a picturesque air to the previously austere boxy structure.

In 1889, the colonel's father died and he inherited the property and a lion's share in the by now highly profitable E.I. du Pont Company. The colonel was president of the Wilmington and Northern Railroad and declined active leadership in the family company. He was, in fact, influential in the sale of the concern to three cousins—Pierre Samuel, T. Coleman, and Alfred I. du Pont—who ultimately built the company into a modern chemical giant. In the process, he became, in 1902, exceedingly prosperous. Without a stern and domineering father looking over his shoulder, he felt free to expand Winterthur again, and converted it into a manor house in the François I style. While maintaining the original house, he added to it an imposing frontispiece, bedecked with stringcourses and balconies, a terra-cotta cornice, and a richly textured Spanish tile roof. Elaborated dormers punctured the roof line and tall chimneys added a skyward thrust. A broad porte-cochère greeted guests, who then entered a grand marble stair hall. With this new wing, the accumulated trappings of landed gentry were in place: billiard room, library, squash court, and a grand reception room in Italian renaissance style with beamed ceiling and red damask wall coverings. In the older part of the house, two rooms were reworked into a Louis XVI parlor and the dining room was enlarged.

The colonel had busied himself with the operation and improvement

*Winterthur from the northeast (opposite), showing the 1902 addition put on the north front by Henry Algernon du Pont. This François I wing was designed by Robeson Lea Perot and Elliston Perot Bissell of Philadelphia. The White Room (above), now the Empire Parlor, was decorated in the Louis XVI style, which was considered appropriate for a formal reception room at the turn of the century*

of the property and farms for several decades. Between 1885 and 1925 he added nine hundred acres to his holdings. By 1918, the farm boasted 1,446 acres of cleared land. Farming operations included meadows for the grazing of his herd of Holstein cattle, which replaced the Devon herd that Bidermann had developed, and cropland to supply his table. There were also 430 acres of woodland that the colonel, like his forebears, relished and protected. Family papers contain numerous references to the agony of losing ancient specimen trees, and to the protective measures, including the installation of lightning rods in the taller examples, that were established. Old trees in the immediate vicinity of the house were especially beloved; well-developed shrubs were equally guarded. At one moment the colonel announced in triumph that he had been able to preserve a euonymus by the edge of the house that was under construction, and at another time he feared that the nearby railroad would disturb the roots of a favored tree.

Just as the expansion of the house was being completed, Mrs. du Pont died. This event and the colonel's election to the U.S. Senate in 1906 put the stewardship of Winterthur increasingly in the hands of the colonel's only son, Henry Francis du Pont, a man who by temperament and training was as perfectly suited to the job as he was capable.

Henry Francis du Pont's childhood at Winterthur had been nearly idyllic. He inherited his family's love of nature and he roamed the property, discovering the hidden natural treasures of its woodlands, collecting mineral specimens and bird eggs, and forming an affection for nature and a love of plants and flowers that remained his lifelong passion. The icy formality of a military father—stern and uncompromising—and the dot-

*Winterthur from the southeast (opposite) after the new roof was added, c. 1884. Henry Francis du Pont and his sister, Louise Evelina, are posed on the south lawn. Henry Francis and Louise Evelina with their mother, Pauline Foster du Pont (above left), c. 1890. Henry Francis du Pont (above), c. 1887, during the years he was roaming the fields and forests of Winterthur and developing his love of the farm, woodlands, and gardens*

71

ing affections of a mother who had buried five of her seven children must certainly have had psychological consequences. His older sister once recalled that if either of them could not remember the Latin name of a plant when asked by their father they were sent to bed without dinner. Not surprisingly, the life on the farm and in the fields, meadows, and gardens provided a welcome relief from the hermetic and stuffy interiors of the house. Du Pont befriended the farmworkers and gardeners and greenhousemen, helped them in their work, and acquired his first practical experience in gardening and husbandry. Sociable but shy, he had a slight speech impediment that reinforced his shyness. His disciplined upbringing fostered that tendency, turning it into a dignified reserve that would dominate his adult personality.

His childhood idyll was shattered when he was sent to Groton in 1893. Situated in a small central Massachusetts town, the all-male college preparatory school was founded by the Reverend Endicott Peabody with the intention of fostering strong minds and strong bodies and promoting the Christian ethic. Du Pont was a fish out of water, especially when compared to such affable and athletic schoolmates as Franklin D. Roosevelt. He was there, by his father's command, to become "a good, useful, honourable man appreciating the duty he owes to the community in which he lives and to his fellow men." The left-handed du Pont was made to use his right by Peabody, a move that modern psychologists believe can have a devastating impact on the individual. Although desperately homesick, du Pont found solace in recalling the beauties of Winterthur, about which he often wrote in his daily notes home, and in frequent visits to a local

greenhouse, where he bought flowers to ornament his room and to cheer sick and despondent companions. He haunted the greenhouse and continued his amateur education in plantsmanship. In early spring, he found parcels of lilies of the valley sent along with the flowers his mother had presented to Mrs. Peabody. There was a regular commerce in spring blossoms packed in damp moss which went as tokens of friendship from the du Ponts to friends within reach of rail lines.

Du Pont was continually challenged to succeed. His father enjoined him, saying, "Never forget that the du Ponts are not accustomed to take back seats and that you have a family reputation to maintain." An undistinguished student, he nonetheless entered Harvard in 1899 with advanced standing that allowed him to conclude his studies in three years. His father's words were probably still ringing in his ears when he wrote home after two years and requested permission to enroll in a horticultural program offered by Harvard at a now defunct branch called the Bussey Institution. The Bussey was located in Jamaica Plain, near Boston, adjacent to the Arnold Arboretum, both having been established through the bequest of Benjamin Bussey. The arboretum was a pioneering horticultural preserve that was founded in 1872 and administered by Charles Sprague Sargent.

As a publicist for the development of a native school of ornamental horticulture, Sargent would have a wide influence on the look of American gardens in general and Winterthur specifically. A description in the magazine *Country Life in America* of his own garden at his estate, HolmLea, in Brookline strikes a familiar chord when one looks at Winterthur today:

*The dining room (opposite), now the Chinese Parlor, included family portraits and a set of New York federal-period dining chairs originally owned by Victor Marie du Pont. Winterthur from the March Walk (above), showing the woody setting and naturalized plantings. The curving drive to the left was altered later, after 1931, when du Pont developed new landscaping for the wing he had added*

73

"Big masses of large flowers ordinarily produce a feeling of show, extravagance, pretense. This garden is artistic because it is a series of dissolving pictures, the views changing every step or two...." This work was indebted to the color approach to gardening pioneered in England by Gertrude Jekyll, but Sargent and others hoped to Americanize it and develop a national school of horticulture.

Sargent was a leader in the recording of native species. He also pioneered in the importation of new plant introductions, amassing as broad ranging a collection as possible at the arboretum. His pioneering interest in Kurume azaleas had a lasting impact on Winterthur; he also had a horticultural personality that du Pont would have found sympathetic. The author of the description above attributed to self-restraint the ultimate success of Sargent's garden: "It is this self-restraint that gives to all his gardening an air of easy grace, so that everything seems to grow for him without effort. He will not crowd flowers even in a spring garden, and that is one reason why his estate is my standard of dignity, permanence, economy, and beauty." Although du Pont probably did not meet Sargent while he was a student, he roamed the Arnold and absorbed its lessons.

Boston in those days was the source of much excitement in the horticultural world. One of the earliest experiments in a public landscaped garden was the founding of Mount Auburn Cemetery in 1831. The Boston area continued to be a center of horticultural experimentation. By the turn of the century it was a virtual hotbed of activity, according to recent research by Winterthur garden historian Valencia Libby. In addition to the Bussey and the Arnold, Harvard had a major herbarium and library complex and a botanical garden with unusual species. The most important landscape designer in America, Frederick Law Olmsted, was a resident of Brookline, where his firm was located. Olmsted and his firm were, in fact, creating most of the major park systems in America, including the "emerald necklace" that was to encircle Boston. In Cambridge, at the Massachusetts Institute of Technology, the first collegiate school of architecture had been founded in 1870 and M.I.T. had become the center for the study of landscape architecture. In 1901, the first Boston Flower Show was held at Horticultural Hall, stimulating much local excitement.

There could not have been a more fertile environment for Henry Francis du Pont to further his interest, and it is clear that his student years were an important period of coalescence of early experiences. He had built a strong visual background and personal response, not only at Winterthur but also through visits to other family members who were equally proud of their gardening activities. At the Bussey, which taught the practical sides of agriculture and horticulture for individuals who intended careers in garden and landscape management, du Pont was exposed to the regimen associated with horticultural practice and gained the systematic knowledge with which to temper his emotional response. He was exposed to a wide range of plant material and developed an appetite for novelties and exotic specimens. Advanced horticultural taste in America was still strongly under English influence, and through his course work he was exposed to the literature of the field and to color theories as applied to garden design. He would soon see these theories at work not only in Pro-

fessor Sargent's garden but also on annual European pilgrimages that he began soon after leaving Harvard.

During these years, du Pont met Marian Cruger Coffin, who was a student at M.I.T. in landscape architecture and whose family had long been friends of the du Ponts. Coffin became a lifelong friend, correspondent, companion on garden pilgrimages, and adviser. Only slightly older than du Pont, she differed principally in her architectural orientation in garden work by being more concerned with spatial designs and by her structural approach to garden sequences. Together they formed their taste and talked comfortably about their ideas and theories, testing judgments and conclusions. Ultimately, Coffin was responsible for landscape design work at Winterthur and through du Pont's introduction was actively employed on numerous garden designs in Delaware.

When Henry Francis du Pont returned to Winterthur after his mother's death, he assumed responsibility for the gardens, although his father was still actively involved in landscape decisions as well. The two appear to have operated quite separately and it is likely that while the younger du Pont was concerned with plant trials and developing new schema for the terraced formal gardens below the house, the elder du Pont was concerned with larger landscape issues and trees and shrub plantings.

With the colonel's expansion of the house in 1902, something grander than the two small greenhouses and beds for the production of flowers, herbs, fruit, and vegetables for the house was required. The greenhouses were relocated and the old garden area developed into a series of terraced gardens. This area provided a restricted formal stage upon which many experiments were tried in the next decades. Plants here were regularly in-

*North facade of Winterthur, 1908, from the March bank with naturalized daffodils*

75

troduced and pulled up when the sequences of their bloom or the shade of their blossoms proved inconsistent with the orderly visual parade the young du Pont envisioned. It was here also that he tested his theories of massing plants of the same or closely related hue that would be mirrored in the floral arrangements used in the house. An observer described the terrace features: "a small pool and two garden houses with an arbor-covered wall fountain between them....The two lower terraces, which comprised the area of the Bidermann's sunken garden, were separated by three arbors of wisteria. One of these terraces was devoted to lawn and wide herbaceous borders of delphinium, poppies, peonies, foxgloves, and similar plantings, with a few pear trees for their flowering effect; the other was a rose garden, with a lily pool at its east end and a fence separating the whole area from the meadow."

With a grander front entrance to the house, the dense woods opposite were thinned and new drives developed. The woods opposite the entry were a perfect theater for naturalizing experiments and du Pont was soon at work laying out sequences of spring bulbs that stagger the imagination in their intricacy and quantity. These plantings were to become a significant feature of the landscape work at Winterthur and their origins certainly go back to du Pont's childhood infatuation with the wildflowers he discovered on the property. No passages more effectively summarize du Pont's approach to the development of the terraced and woodland gardens than those in two letters discovered by Valencia Libby and written by du Pont when he was detained in Paris and unable to return to Winterthur to supervise the autumn planting of 1911. "Can you believe my

*Dairy barns built in 1918. Henry Francis assumed responsibility for farm operations in 1914 and greatly expanded the herd and advanced the breeding*

being here at this writing, when I ought to be superintending this very minute the planting of all those lovely tulips to be?" he questioned, barely concealing his frustration. "By some divine Providence I had a painstaking lady landscape architect [Elizabeth Colwell, Marian Coffin's assistant] make a detailed planting plan of the garden in tulip season last Spring, and—much to her consternation and, I feel sure, secret rage—I made her note with greatest accuracy the position of each tulip. In fear and trembling I sent her a letter some time ago stating that inasmuch as she had made such an admirable plan, I felt sure she would be quite equal to the superintending of the planting of the tulips, but I am steeling myself already for some rude shocks next Spring."

The "lady landscape architect" was not the only one so charged. Du Pont also commandeered a cousin, Anna Robinson, into the woods to supervise the wild plantings. In a letter which upon opening young Anna must surely have trembled at, he entreated: "I should be very grateful if you would undertake to superintend the planting of these bulbs by Nicholas. All you need to do is to walk over the sloping bank looking for wooden labels with names corresponding to those on the list and, in addition, September 1911 written on them. Should there be four or five labels with the same name, what you must do is give the package of those bulbs to Nicholas and say, 'Here are the bulbs; they must be divided into two, three, or four lots,' as the question may be, and then show him where the places are. I find it is not safe to give him one lot until the one previously given him is planted." The prospect seems easy enough until one realizes that planting bulbs among the matted roots of trees is difficult at best, and when one is trying to avoid digging up already positioned bulbs of various sizes the project takes on complicated dimensions. The number of bulbs involved in the 1911 plantings is not recorded; in 1909 du Pont ordered 25,000 bulbs and in 1913 the number had risen to 39,000. Anna must have known that whatever errors emerged would be laid at her doorstep. The instructions continued: "After the bulbs are planted I wish you would leave my labels in as they are, simply tying on another wooden label with 'Anna' written on it. If, by some mistake, there should not be enough bulbs to fill the required spaces, simply omit planting one of them but kindly mention the fact on a little label. The bank, of course, in addition to the spaces marked is full of labels of bulbs that are already planted there, and naturally these must not be disturbed." Anna's response at the termination of her duties: "the relief is intense...."

The decisions Henry Francis du Pont made regarding the naturalized specimens were systematic and logical, and at the same time were overlaid with a response to the terrain and a desire to let nature speak its own voice. In developing the March Walk, as it came to be known, he had planted thousands of bulbs, carefully intermixing different types so as to maximize the blooming season and guarantee a graceful transition from one blooming sequence to the next. The actual disposition of the bulbs was determined by placing irregular tree branches on the ground and using their profiles as a guide to patterned irregularity. For larger drifts of naturalized bulbs, the same planting method was employed. However, the bulbs used were carefully experimented with, screened, and then laid out in rows in testing gardens before their introduction into the woods and fields. Although, clearly, they were meant to be seen en masse, each variety was analyzed for color and shape. Subtle decisions such as the preference of small cupped narcissus for woodlands and larger blossomed varieties for meadow plantings were involved in every element of the garden work.

Du Pont approached the planning and planting of a garden with the precision of a military tactician. He made voluminous notes on his own plant trials as well as on varieties seen in other gardens with possible suggestions as to where they might be usefully employed at Winterthur. On daily walks through the garden, he recorded growth and blossoming habits with the fervor of a parent measuring each advance of childhood. His garden notebooks are crammed with observations on height, size, color, and intensity. In addition to annual garden pilgrimages abroad, he carried on a correspondence with greenhouses, magazines, horticulturists, and friends in his search of a specimen, a cutting, a supply source, or a hint as to growth habits or culture methods. A typical instance is a note to his trusted adviser and friend Bertha Benkard, who was instrumental in the planning and implementation of the collections. "I wonder if your man, by any chance, is a friend of W. R. Coe's gardener, because I would give my eye teeth and considerable cash besides for one or two cuttings of the double orange Hibiscus he just showed at the horticultural show which was held in the Natural History Museum last week." The purpose of all of this work was to create a personal and masterful garden composition, coaxing as much sustained beauty as possible from the available material. His plantings were organized to be visually pleasing and to bloom at calculated intervals to guarantee the success of his color schemes. To fill in the gaps left from spring bulbs gone by, he adopted for many years the Victorian idea of bedding out; that is, filling in vacant spaces with thousands of annuals.

Although his first work at Winterthur was focused on the formal gardens and naturalized beds, as time passed his field of vision enlarged. Broad landscape effects became an increasing concern, especially after his father's election to the Senate took the elder du Pont to Washington for extended stays. Possibly under the influence of Charles Sprague Sargent, who had an intense interest in azaleas and rhododendrons, du Pont had acquired azaleas as early as 1906, generally for forcing to ornament the house. Du Pont became fascinated in the possibilities of developing an azalea plantation. A revival of interest in the Orient in the early twentieth century had brought new oriental plantings into American gardens. A special flurry of excitement surrounded the arrival of a group of Kurume azaleas shown at the Panama-Pacific Exposition in San Francisco in 1915. These specimens were purchased by Cottage Gardens in New Jersey, where they were spied by du Pont. The humble beginnings of the most spectacular horticultural display at Winterthur, the Azalea Woods, was modestly recorded by du Pont: "I told Mr. Brown I would take these seventeen plants and practically all the Kurumes I have naturalized in our woods are cuttings from them. The Chestnut Blight had left many openings, and before I knew it Robertson, our Scottish gardener, had numerous young Kurume plants with no place to go except the woods, where they have been ever since." Needless to say, what is left out of this abbreviated chronicle is all the intense testing, planting, and repositioning that characterized all the other garden work.

By 1914, Henry Francis du Pont had also taken on responsibility for the farm operations at Winterthur and he brought to this activity the same energy and enthusiasm he had invested in his gardening activity. Continuing the family tradition of experimental and scientific agriculture begun by his great-grandfather more than a century before, he immediately set to work to improve the herd of Holstein-Friesian cattle with which his father had replaced Bidermann's Devon herd. His experiments in inbreeding led to improved strains and national recognition. After 1922, when the Holstein-Friesian Association instituted an annual honor list for Breeder, Owner, and Sire, Winterthur appeared regularly on it until 1950. For more than twenty-two years, Winterthur Farms was leading Honor List Owner and Breeder seventeen times, and during nineteen years made a grand-slam winning in all three categories eleven times. To support this activity, du Pont experimented with advanced farm machinery and built model barns for the dairy herd.

In gardening and in farming, Henry Francis du Pont became an innovator and a leader. In pursuing these interests, he was part of a movement to rescue the rural environment from the threat of urbanization and to promote a country-house culture based on well-established English models.

Critics and reformers from the middle of the nineteenth century had been extolling the virtues of rural life over the often drab and enervating existence in the city. The rural world was considered healthier than the city, and for many people it was also thought to be an environment that promoted the basic values upon which the nation had been constructed. The rise of the city was not greeted universally as a mark of progress, and the smoke-belching factories and arduous labor associated with mills and manufactories were cited as further evidence of the inhumanity implicit in the advance of machine technology. Not surprisingly, the first powerful voice espousing the amenity of country living and seeking to find in the countryside the models for an honest American architectural style was a landscape gardener, Andrew Jackson Downing. As the publisher of *The Horticulturalist,* Downing created a popular movement to rework the landscape of the American countryside, and through a series of equally popular books on landscape gardening and rural architecture he enshrined rural life as an antidote to the venality and degradation of the city. Downing and his followers succeeded in awakening many Americans to rural virtues; they also succeeded in popularizing rural architectural styles whose picturesque massing and playful ornament was in sympathy with their landscape theories. They helped defeat the tyranny of the neoclassical styles that had dominated American architecture for the first several decades of the nineteenth century.

Country houses, often built to escape summer's heat and epidemics of crowded cities, had existed since the eighteenth century in America; by the mid-nineteenth century, the enshrinement of rural amenities had sparked the rise of picturesque suburbs and the plantation of rural landscape gardens in the form of public parks in the midst of cities. The

American park movement owes its origins to many of the same forces that created the country house culture.

The railroad and, subsequently, the streetcar made living a distance from work feasible. Frequent trips abroad for the well-to-do brought the pleasures of country house living into sharp focus. Increased capital and leisure and an already established vogue for vast seaside homes provided a strong impetus to the cause of country living. Furthermore, there was an enviable model in the English tradition of rural estates and the centuries-old development of country house living. For the newly ennobled American capitalists such lifestyles and the social acceptance they betokened had a clear appeal.

Native architects and designers, boasting professional beaux-arts training and an enlarged vision as the result of extensive travel, and well-developed libraries and files crammed with photographs of European buildings to serve as a source of design ideas and details were ready for the task at hand. Large offices of draftsmen were capable of producing the complicated plans required not only for this sort of enterprise but also for the generation of skyscrapers they were in the process of creating, often for the same patron. Optimism was boundless and commissions flowed in. Landscape gardening had become similarly professional and with dedicated energy designers described vast terraced gardens and acres of park landscape as the necessary embellishments to a great country place. Box-lined allées, reflecting pools and bubbling fountains, sundial gardens, arbors, even grottoes and temples now dotted the landscape. From the Berkshires, Vermont, and Connecticut, to Pennsylvania and the deep reaches of rural Long Island, the countryside virtually teemed with country seats, a few hours distant from urban centers and readily accessible by the miles of railroad tracks that now laced the northeastern corner of the nation.

Magazines extolling the pleasures of country life such as *House and Garden* or *The House Beautiful*, which explored with new energy the logical and exciting relationship between house and grounds, poured off the presses. It is not surprising that the prestigious English magazine *Country Life* began producing an American edition or that it rapidly found its way into the library at Winterthur. Yet Winterthur was different from many of the country homes. The gardening, the farming, and the architectural improvements were all the thoughtful products of the owners, and the property had had a long and continuous history of ownership and improvement by the same family. The family was different also, more closely knit than others of similar wealth and unlike their contemporaries who traced their wealth to rural communities but moved away, the du Ponts kept their roots firmly placed at Winterthur. What made Winterthur unique among the hundreds of other country places developed around the same time was the ultimate dedication of the house to a great collection that in becoming public has become one of the most important museums of American art in the country. The fact that these innovations in horticulture, breeding, and collecting can be ascribed to a single individual makes the impact of his achievements just that much more profound.

*The scale and proportions of the hall and parlor
from Port Royal, a 1762 house built near Philadelphia, provide a handsome introduction to Winterthur and a lavish setting for masterworks from
·the collection. The hall (above), with its finely
scaled doric entablature, fielded dado, graceful
fanlights, and wide doorways, gives an impressive
vista into the garden. Three New York slab tables
and a boldly scaled Philadelphia arched-back sofa
covered in an English chintz whose natural motifs coordinate with the hand-painted eighteenth-
century Chinese wallpaper complement the hall*

Eighteenth-century notions of symmetry, balance, and order are evident in the use of classical architectural ornament and furniture arranged in pairs or sets. Prosperity and reason are the simultaneous messages of the great public rooms at Winterthur, here the Port Royal Hall (left) and Port Royal Parlor (above). This is seen in the rich burl and gilt carving of a pair of mirrors that hung in the Beacon Street (Boston) home of Abigail Phillips, who married Josiah Quincy in 1769, and in the handsome restraint of the matched pair of sofas that belonged to John Dickinson, patriot and author of Letters from a Farmer in Pennsylvania (1768). Lively embellishments lend

a rococo air to the restrained forms of Philadelphia high chests, which are also arranged symmetrically. The Gratz family high chest seen against the far wall has a matching dressing table and is counterpointed by the Van Pelt family high chest (not shown) on the opposite wall. Rich carving ornaments the nearly two dozen chairs and tables, mostly of Philadelphia origin, which form a lexicon of Chippendale design and fill out the ample dimension of this stately room in perfect symmetrical arrangement

Across the Port Royal Hall, a suite of rooms from Readbourne, built around 1733 in Queen Anne's County, Maryland, displays furniture in the Queen Anne style, which immediately preceded Chippendale in America. Organized to show the period practice of placing a phalanx of chairs against the wall to be brought into the center of a room as needed, Readbourne Stair Hall (above and opposite top) also shows the simpler architectural tendency of the second quarter of the eighteenth century. The arched opening leads to a stairway that reaches to the upper stories of the house and mirrors the arched niche filled with a graduated set of Chinese export porcelain bowls

assembled individually by Mr. du Pont. The preference for large volumes and full curves that dominated the Queen Anne style is evident in the supple contours of the Philadelphia chairs with their cabriole legs, horseshoe-shaped seats, curved splats, and rounded crest rails. The chairs form a perfect amalgam of the "s," or cyma curve, which was identified by the English painter William Hogarth as the line of beauty. Hogarth painted dramatic and literary subjects in addition to the staple of portraiture. The work of such native Americans as Robert Feke (above) and John Singleton Copley (opposite top) and of such itinerant Englishmen as John Wollaston (right) came

exclusively from portrait commissions. These
painters found no patronage in the colonies for
more ambitious work. Painting was often no more
than an ornamental trade, and house and sign
painters turned their skill to graining and mar-
bleizing or, at their most sophisticated level, to the
intricate work of Japanning, as seen on the Pimm
high chest installed in Readbourne Parlor (left).
Its simulated tortoise-shell decoration is enlivened with gessoed and gilt designs of animals
and oriental figures derived from Chinese painting and taken from one of the popular craftsmen's manuals

Paneling from Readbourne, painted a pale yellow
typical of the palette favored at the end of the
eighteenth century, sheaths the walls of the
Du Pont Dining Room (above and opposite) directly above Port Royal Parlor. The furnishings of
the federal period present a distinct break with
the rococo Chippendale style that preceded it.
Richly figured woods arranged in flat geometrical
fields, contrasting bands of inlay, classical trophies, and an overall rectilinear form of the furnishings replace the sculptural carving and deep-
toned richness of the earlier style. Despite wartime deprivation and efforts at restricting America's maritime activity, trade flourished, and with it
new regional styles sprang up. The sideboard
made in Newburyport, Massachusetts, like others

in the dining room from Newport and New York,
supports an extravagant display of American
glass and silver, serving pieces, and ornamental
urns of Chinese export porcelain. The three-part
dining table, inlaid at the top of the legs with an
American eagle, is over twelve feet long at full extension and is surrounded by a large set of New
York chairs acquired about 1800 by Victor Marie
du Pont, the brother of Eleuthère Irénée. French
and English imports flooded the market after the
American Revolution and put great competitive
pressure on American manufacturers. The English
transfer-printed dinner service on the table and
the yellow and silver lusterware in the Salem secretary
bookcase are characteristic of such imports

# THE COLLECTOR IN AMERICA

In the world of country houses and in the habits and rituals of the elite society he inhabited, Henry Francis du Pont was very much at home. Despite his lonely childhood and isolation in school, he adapted to the demands placed upon him. Perhaps it was the specter of his father's injunction not to take a back seat or simply his curiosity and interest in everything he encountered that helped him to move freely in his world. Out of wide-ranging contacts he made devoted and lifelong friends. As a student at Harvard he attended dances, teas, and other social events in Boston. His already-married sister, Louise, lived in nearby Marblehead. Her husband, Frank Crowninshield, a descendant of an ancient New England family with extensive connections, was a man of strong political sentiments and an active disposition. Through his sister, du Pont's circle of friends and contacts expanded and his invitations multiplied. It is also probable that his sister influenced his early collecting. It was during his student years that he made his first antiques purchase, a pair of delft cows that he kept in his room at Harvard. Frank Crowninshield's cousin Edward was the first dealer in Chinese export porcelain in America and also had a formative influence on du Pont.

The serious collection of antiques was still decades away for Henry Francis du Pont. There remained much of the world to discover. Trips to Europe during his youth had already exposed him to foreign customs and attuned him to the variety and wonder of the history of art. After his return to Winterthur from school he undertook regular trips abroad, often spending from May to October in foreign capitals and touring the countryside. Churches, museums, country houses, and gardens—always gar-

*Increasing trade with the Far East inspired a popular taste for oriental motifs in the decorative arts of the eighteenth century. The Chinese Parlor (opposite) was carved out of two rooms in the original (1839) Winterthur house and provides a transition between the 1928–31 wing and the 1902 wing. A complete set of hand-painted wallpaper details life and leisure in a Chinese village and shows garden landscapes. Chinese fretworks, pagoda forms, and other such exotic influences are worked into the ornaments of the Chippendale furniture in this room*

Entrance Hall of the 1902 wing (opposite) before the marble and iron staircase was removed and the Montmorenci staircase was installed in the mid-1930's. The false beams and overstuffed furniture of the Red Room (left) were typical of the gloomy atmosphere du Pont disliked in his father's house. This room at the western end of the 1902 addition was replaced by the Marlboro Room in 1934

dens—were examined, analyzed, and mastered. Wherever possible he met and befriended the great horticulturists and regularly visited nurseries, ordering extensively for Winterthur and sometimes transporting his purchases back with him. Even as he fled England in 1914 with the threat of war looming, he wrote hurriedly to Ellen Willmott to try and secure some last specimens before sailing. On at least one of his garden pilgrimages in Europe he was accompanied by Marian Coffin.

At Winterthur he lived the role of squire of the manor, overseeing the estate and consulting with the chief gardener or the foreman of the farm but always finally investigating for himself as well, supervising at close hand to make sure that everything met his exacting specifications.

Social life at Winterthur was sophisticated and lavish. The family was proud of its French heritage and employed French servants, addressing them in their native tongue. The colonel had, in fact, long considered himself the family genealogist and historian and maintained an active communication with relatives abroad. Through these relationships, business and social associations, and the colonel's activities in Washington the family circle of international contacts expanded.

An engaging glimpse of Winterthur at the turn of the century is provided by Marian Lawrence, a friend of Louise Crowninshield who came to visit in 1905. She arrived by train in Wilmington but through an oversight was not met at the station. She took a cab to the tollhouse on the Kennett Turnpike, where she was met by a horse-drawn station wagon from Winterthur driven by a liveried servant. "The rest of the way we flew," she recorded. "I never saw a horse go so fast unless he was running away." (Fast horses, fast cars, and pioneering aviation captivated various du Pont men, and Henry Francis du Pont always had a passion for big cars. At one time he sported a 16-cylinder Cadillac.) Lawrence continued her chronicle:

> We came to an iron gate which sprang open for us mysteriously and after what seemed an endless avenue through very tall trees, drew up at a huge porte-cochere and in it was Louise waiting for me. The house seemed enormous! The halls solid marble with marble pillars and staircases with bronze railings all the way up to the third story. Large azalea trees in full bloom were set about in the hall in pots.

She was at Winterthur at the perfect time—spring—and although young du Pont had only been working on the grounds for three years, his influence was already felt. On the following morning, May 9, Lawrence continued her account:

> Waked to a gorgeous day. I have two large windows in my room opening out onto a balcony and the sounds of birds and scent of flowers that came floating in were quite intoxicating after a long northern winter. Harry Dupont, Louise's nice young brother, asked me to go to drive and we drove for an hour or more without going off their grounds. His father was in New York so he is now the boss and he stopped to speak to the workmen. There are two or three hundred working on the place all the time doing and undoing the orders of the Colonel. Frank says they build a terrace of solid masonry and then the Colonel decides it would look better a few inches to the right or left so they do it all over again. It makes me sad to see so much money wasted with such poor results; but the woods and fields full of flowers were a delight. Shimmering white dogwood grew thick amongst the tall trees, and azaleas and Judas trees made a colorful underbrush. Harry Dupont told me to pick all the lilies of the valley I liked, write the addresses of people to whom I wanted them sent and the butler would box and send them. This is a luxury! I picked until I was tired and sent them to the family and aunts at home.

A round of visits and dinners followed with a mixture of titled visitors, local worthies, and family. After one meal while most of the visitors sat down to play bridge, a ritual that would survive unabated during Henry du Pont's tenure, the colonel showed Marian Lawrence the library, or, to be more exact, "every book in his library and I thought I should go crazy admiring them one by one." Through visits and entertainments such as these, du Pont became accustomed to the social calendar that would rule life at Winterthur for the remainder of his occupancy.

In 1916, Henry Francis du Pont married Ruth Wales, a New Yorker with a deep love of music. Ruth du Pont was an amiable companion and shared her husband's love of travel, although she did not often accompany him on his antiquing expeditions. She enjoyed country life and entertaining but left most decisions regarding the furnishings and running of the various du Pont houses to her husband. She devoted much of her time to raising their two children, Pauline Louise and Ruth Ellen. One of her passions was bridge, at which she spent many hours. The du Ponts eventually took an apartment in New York City and spent increasingly longer periods of time away from Winterthur, either traveling or simply engaging in the

*Installation view of the Girl Scouts Loan Exhibition, New York City, 1929. Henry Francis du Pont was a major lender and organized the displays into roomlike settings. Prominent in this view of the "Dining Room" is the eight-legged New York sideboard that is a feature of the Du Pont Dining Room at Winterthur today*

more active social life of New York. Henry Francis still supervised the farm and garden operations, often journeying there alone for brief periods to check over the place, but he had begun to exercise greater independence. Winterthur became his country place, an alternative rather than a full-time residence. His attention turned to his own home in New York and to the collecting of English and French antiques to furnish it. While he had been highly individual in his approach to gardening and farming, in his furnishings he followed accepted taste.

The taste for European furniture was deeply embedded by this period. With the rise of the great millionaires' mansions and a more authoritative approach to the correctness of their design in a particular style vocabulary, the furniture designed for these houses was also more correct. In addition, some of the great collections of European decorative arts were being formed during this period in Europe and America. Architects ransacked Europe for antique furniture and architectural details to incorporate into their designs, and the movement toward a refined European taste was given a further positive thrust by the publication of Edith Wharton and Ogden Codman's book, *The Decoration of Houses*. For these publicists and a host of other commentators, European furniture suggested a refinement of taste and a well-mannered nobility they perceived to be lacking in American life. Compared to the urbane and cosmopolitan European counterparts, Americans appeared boorish and clumsy. Social commentators advocated refinements in Americans' surroundings as a way of creating an ennobling influence. With such strident and aristocratic attitudes it is easy to see how the simple productions of the colonial era escaped serious notice.

During the nineteenth century there had, of course, been pioneer spirits, American boosters who took a profound interest in the country's past, but this consciousness was largely political and historic. The arts of early America were valued primarily as curiosities or rare patriotic survivals. Ancestral portraits and single objects associated with historic individuals were objects of veneration and were preserved and occasionally pulled out and displayed in connection with a historic occasion or anniversary observance. The images of the nation's founders had always possessed a magical authority and had an iconic value in the culture; it is not surprising that such portraits were the first to find their way into art museums. As shrines of the early republic, the homes of those same individuals had been the center of the earliest episodes in the historic preservation movement in America; however, the interest was not in the design and architecture of the buildings but in their former inhabitants. The fight waged by Ann Pamela Cunningham and her Mount Vernon Ladies Association in 1856 proved a remarkable example of grass-roots preservation at a time when the gathering clouds of sectional conflict seemed to be undermining the foundations on which the country had been built. Revivals of interest in American arts often paralleled emerging uncertainties about the current state of the country or reflected increased pressures on the social and political fabric from some outside force.

Historic architecture stood in the way of urban development. If a historic home had been fortunate enough to escape the ravages of the fires that frequently devastated historic urban centers, it could not escape the

pressure of development. Furniture and pictures, on the other hand, could be put in the attic or the barn or relegated to a back room for use. Such historic artifacts also became the quarry for the generally eccentric individuals who as early as the late eighteenth century began collecting material remains of America's past. During the nineteenth century, countless historical societies were established, especially in New England, where more than nine hundred exist today. These organizations fostered the first examination of the chronicle of American life and willingly accepted objects with local or associational interest or as merely quaint curiosities.

By the period of the centennial of American independence in 1876, a new approach to early objects began to appear. While still valued largely for their historic content or because they provided a measure for current progress, American antiques began, haltingly, to be analyzed and viewed for their aesthetic qualities. This movement was influenced by the emerging generation of design reformers who felt that mechanization had robbed life of its virtue. The reformers saw in the products of older craft traditions visible evidence of the close connection between the craftsman and his work, and found an integrity of design as the evidence of that connection. The man who operated a machine had lost that intimate contact with his product, which as a result was robbed of its human dimension. The Arts and Crafts movement, as it is commonly known, did much for the revival of interest in early objects that were seen as the product of the happy craftsman, totally in harmony with his universe, who created workmanlike goods rather than the shoddy wares stamped out by the machine. The crafts of the middle ages, less highly finished than later objects

*Henry Francis and Ruth Wales du Pont with their daughters, Pauline Louise and Ruth Ellen, 1922*

95

*Armchair (above) from New York City
or western Long Island, 1670–90. Oak.
Height: 42½." Spice cabinet or case of
boxes (above right) from Salem, Massachusetts, 1676. Red oak. Height: 17¼."
Chest of drawers (right) from Ipswich,
Massachusetts, 1678. Red oak, poplar,
maple, walnut. Height: 42"*

and therefore bearing visible testimony of the craft process, were especially prized.

The nineteenth century had a romance with history and with distant epochs and alien cultures. It is not surprising, given the rise of ro-
manticism in this period and the fascination with the gothic novel,
picturesque narratives, and macabre tales, that serious attention was paid
to the era of the Puritan settlement. Not only did the Pilgrim Fathers possess an eerie fascination for Americans at this time but their migration to
America had set in motion the foundations of modern America. Pilgrim-
century furniture, with its flat decorative carving, robust proportions,
strongly grained woods, and direct construction methods, best reflected the
concerns for honesty in furniture that were espoused by such reformers
as Clarence Cook, whose influential volume, *The House Beautiful*, was published at the time of the centennial. Cook mirrored the aesthetic doctrines
set forth a decade earlier in England by Charles Locke Eastlake, an apol-
ogist for medieval styles. American followers recognized the underlying
medievalism in Pilgrim-century furniture, and Cook illustrated a number of examples of work of this period as exemplars of honest design. Cook
also included illustrations of eighteenth-century work and encouraged the
search for American antiques in response to the decline of taste he perceived in contemporary work and in factory production.

The first generation of dedicated collectors of American furniture
and antiques appeared in New England during the closing decades of the
nineteenth century. There had been sporadic interest earlier but this period witnessed a coalescence of interest that laid the foundations for a

sustained tradition. New England was a fertile hunting ground. Conservative taste had led to the preservation of early objects that were often found in rural houses and small towns, away from urban centers and therefore less threatened by the fires that frequently devastated city centers or the equally destructive operation of fashionable taste that condemned outmoded objects to the junkman. There was, in addition, a strong sense of history and commitment to the maintenance of traditions inherited directly from earlier generations.

The New England collectors were not people of extreme wealth but were comfortably affluent professionals with education and dedication, a taste for history, and an idea that American objects had a value beyond their history. They felt these objects provided silent testimony to the positive side of American society and culture. These collectors were also the first individuals to seriously study the history of American antiques, and they sought out and recorded the stories and documents associated with these objects from owners who were, in some cases, only a generation removed from their creation. Furniture is highly mobile and it took the intuition of an archeologist to correctly assign objects to a region or shop tradition. The unlikely chance survival of dated examples in their places of origin, the hazards of memory, and the lack of pictorial records and comparative examples all plagued early students. The objects were not all comfortably deposited in galleries and museum storage rooms but had to be ferreted out, one by one, through legwork, snooping, and cajolery. The monumental task of unraveling the complexities of shop tradition, regional origins and variations, and a stylistic chronology was boldly confronted. Given the fact that the study of American history in general was in its infancy, the early foundation of a workable scholarship for American furniture was an extraordinary accomplishment. It is even more remarkable given the fragile beginnings of that working method that the first detailed examination of American furniture, Dr. Irving W. Lyon's *Colonial Furniture of New England*, is considered today not only a landmark study but an invaluable reference for the scholar.

Scores of books popularizing the subject of colonial furniture, antiques, and interiors would flow from the pens of Alice Morse Earl, Newton Elwell, Esther Singleton, and others. While celebrating the qualities of early work, these volumes often confused the chronicle, attributing forms to the wrong region or style period and making erroneous assertions about the function of certain forms. The confusion of imported versus domestically manufactured objects only added to the problem. Such books perpetrated a highly romanticized vision and promoted antiques on the basis of their quaintness or picturesque attributes. Although the understanding of aesthetic qualities of American design may have been limited, these publications did help to generate a popular enthusiasm for the subject and promoted the concept of the appropriateness of historical American objects in modern interiors.

American museums, for the most part, ignored American objects. The earliest major civic art institutions in New York, Boston, and Philadelphia had only been founded in the decade of the 1870's and were laboring to acquire broadly representative collections of the history of world art. The earliest inroads of American objects into museums were

made in the field of silver. Because of the preciousness of the material, silver had always been highly prized, easily transported, and retained. Silver was frequently preserved as a memento of some family or historical association. The presence of engraved dates, ciphers, or coats of arms, and the frequency of marked objects all added to the documentability of silver. Silver production had responded more rapidly and completely to style changes, since new forms or ornamental languages could be implemented without learning a new craft process, which was often the case with furniture making and its many techniques from veneering to carving to inlay work. Silver bridged the gap into high art and readily found a sympathetic hearing from museum trustees.

The first extensive museum exhibitions of American antiques were silver exhibitions. As early as 1897, the Metropolitan Museum of Art accepted Mrs. Samuel P. Avery's spoon collection. In 1906, the Museum of Fine Arts in Boston put on a show of American silver organized by Francis Hill Bigelow and John R. Buck at the suggestion of Bigelow and R. T. Haines Halsey, who in ensuing years would have a dramatic impact on the display of American antiques in American museums.

In the same year, the Pendleton House was opened in Providence, Rhode Island. A Georgian-style structure loosely based on the home of collector Charles Pendleton was constructed by the Rhode Island School of Design to house Pendleton's collection of American antique furniture, which the school had received two years earlier. The Pendleton collection set a precedent in making available to the public a large group of high-style American furniture whose merits were promoted on an aesthetic and

design basis rather than as antiquarian curiosities. The installation of that collection in rooms whose scale and detailing simulated that of domestic interiors emphasized the functional origins of the forms while suggesting relationships of style language. It also underscored the integrity of the pieces as a collection, thereby also enshrining the persona of the collector. An alternative concept of the period room was explored contemporaneously at the Essex Institute in Salem, Massachusetts. Pioneering director George Francis Dow assembled three vignettes of American furniture that placed heavy emphasis on the use and miscellany that a real room snatched from the context of an individual's daily life might contain. The Essex Institute was a historical association with a century-long history of collecting, while the Rhode Island School of Design, situated in a major manufacturing town, was a practical institution charged with improving the state of industrial design and manufacturing. In an effort to compete with popular European imports, American manufacturers were timidly probing the country's own past for design models.

The display of historic decorative arts as models for study by the designer and craftsman had long been considered by museums an appropriate educational activity. When the Metropolitan Museum was founded in 1870, it numbered among its charter purposes, "The application of arts to manufactures and practical life." The practical reality of this goal was the commitment to wide-ranging decorative arts collections, displayed by culture, period, and material, in endless and uninspiring cases. Such exhibits obscured the cultural background of the objects and their relationship to objects of different material in the same design idiom. The mu-

*Silver two-handled cup with cover (opposite), from New York, 1666–99. Made by Jurian Blanck, Jr. Height: 5⅝." Engraved with the arms of Jacobus and Eve Philipse Van Cortlandt. Silver sugar box (above), c. 1702. Made by Edward Winslow. Width: 7⅜"*

seum's approach was that of the storehouse or repository and only the most dedicated visitor had the patience to wade through the poorly lit galleries in search of self-edification. An elitist spirit was at odds with a democratic ideal.

When, in 1909, the Metropolitan decided to append a section of American arts to an exhibition of Dutch paintings installed to commemorate the Hudson-Fulton celebration—the three hundredth anniversary of Hudson's navigation of that river and the hundredth anniversary of Fulton's steam navigation of the river—the first intention was to exhibit works of Fulton's era. The museum at this point had no American furniture in its collection. The display that was finally installed was more wide ranging chronologically than first planned. The objects were borrowed entirely from the major collectors of the day, which included George S. Palmer, Eugene Bolles, Dwight Blaney, R. T. Haines Halsey, and Henry H. Flagler, among others. In this exhibition lay the seeds of the development of the American Wing. The organizers had a larger purpose in mind—they wanted to test "whether American domestic art was worthy of a place in an art museum, and to test it out not theoretically but visually." The exhibition was enormously popular, and soon after it closed the museum announced the purchase of the Bolles collection with funds provided by Mrs. Russell Sage.

Henry Watson Kent, secretary of the museum and author of many revolutionary and professionalizing advances in museum practice, devised a plan to convince the president of the Metropolitan Museum to commit to American objects. Kent decided to take Mr. and Mrs. deForest and R. T. H. Halsey to New England and to use architectural survivors to encourage an image of the past. Other than the three furnished vignettes they saw at the Essex Institute they would not have found museum installations to serve as models or inspiration. With the acquisition of the Bolles collection, most of the components for future museum and collection developments were in place. Leadership in collecting American furniture was passing out of the hands of the antiquarian and the historical society and into the hands of art museums and collectors.

It would be more than a decade before the American Wing opened at the Metropolitan, and a similar number of years before the first magazine devoted to the interests of collectors would be founded. But enthusiasm was growing. According to Kent:

> The purchase of the Bolles collection in 1909 was the occasion for the founding of the Walpole Society, a group of the most distinguished first collectors of American things—furniture, silver, and what not....Luke Vincent Lockwood, who had written a book on American furniture, and I went on to Boston to conclude the transaction with Bolles, and we handed him a check in the Union Club over a magnum of champagne. Realizing how few collectors of such things at the time knew one another, I proposed the organization of a society so that they might come together, which met with the approval of the others, and we immediately took the necessary steps to bring this about. The first meeting was held in Hartford on January 21, 1910, with twelve gentlemen present....

This small, select group of collectors formed the most significant

corpus of American antiques enthusiasts, suggesting how very limited the serious collecting of American objects was at this time, but the sanction of social acceptability created by this organization did much to further the cause at the personal level. The Walpole Society remained for generations as a bench mark against which American collectors and collecting would be measured. It became the arena for the exchange of ideas and the sharing of information, it organized visits and tours along the eastern seaboard to see collections and sites, and it published scholarly studies and personal reminiscences. It was from among the ranks of the Walpole Society that the organizers of the American Wing would come.

During the second decade of the century, the Metropolitan Museum continued to collect American objects, working toward the eventual creation of permanent galleries. Special exhibitions, including a silver show in 1911 and a Duncan Phyfe exhibition in 1922, confirmed the interest perceived earlier and pushed the field in the direction of scholarly research and connoisseurship. Although museum professionals were still drawn from the ranks of knowledgeable amateurs, the foundations of scholarship were being laid. The process of collecting became increasingly one of analysis, systematization, and interpretation.

Meanwhile, problems confronted the Metropolitan in planning its galleries. The museum probably believed that the simplicity of American furniture would make it look inferior when placed next to the more ornate and sumptuous objects of European craft production and felt that the American objects needed to be seen independently. The museum also felt that although the Hudson-Fulton celebration had been well received, the vast beaux-arts halls of the museum were an unsympathetic environment for the small-scale domestic artifacts of colonial America. The museum already had European period rooms in its collection, and experiments in installing decorative arts in room settings had been successful in Germany and Switzerland. Pendleton House and the Essex Institute also provided useful models. Following these examples it was decided that the American collections would be installed in a separate wing organized on broadly chronological lines. The American Wing was to feature period room settings recalling the domestic interiors of the original owners of high-style objects. Such settings were considered sympathetic to display

*Installation view of the Hudson-Fulton exhibition at the Metropolitan Museum of Art, New York City, 1909*

101

The carved eagles (above) in Schimmel Hall were made by Wilhelm Schimmel, an itinerant Pennsylvania German carver who worked in the Carlisle, Pennsylvania, area from the 1860's to 1890. These carvings were popular with early twentieth-century collectors who had a passion for eagles in all their permutations. The eagle was emblazoned on boxes that contained the wax seal attached to government treaties. This seal box (left) in Empire Hall was made between 1820 and 1860. The French porcelain vase was decorated by Jeroche between 1820 and 1830 and bears a likeness of Lafayette, who made a triumphal tour of America in 1824 recalling his participation in the American Revolution a half-century earlier and helpful in illustrating the relationship of style and workmanship of objects from a region or style period. The interiors were taken from actual houses and arranged around a central gallery space that would provide a more traditional showcase for selected objects. When the American Wing opened in 1924 it created a sensation. Henry Francis du Pont recalled later that it was the great American decorative arts event of the time. And as Kent later reminisced: "The opening of the American Wing, like the Hudson-Fulton exhibition, astonished everybody by the interest and attendance it attracted. Those of us of the staff who had worked hard to bring it about were well repaid. American decorative art had suddenly been put on the map."

That map was, in many ways, as primitive as the first navigational charts that brought the early explorers to American shores. But it was also a broadside, a bold iteration of a set of commonly shared values on the part of the museum's close-knit leadership. They underscored the birthright and ancestry that they felt might be lost by the immigrants displaced by the ravages of World War I and the political and economic upheaval it had engendered. The isolation from Europe caused by the war had forced Americans to fall upon their own resources, and that in turn had given a much-needed lift to the national self-image. As immigrants flooded America with their foreign languages and customs, there seemed to arise a threat to American traditions, and the modern specter of Bolshevism cast a dark and threatening shadow. Something had to be done to limit this threat and to provide for the rapid conversion of the disenfranchised into Americans. Nineteen twenty-four not only saw the opening of the American Wing, it also witnessed the passing of legislation tightening restrictions on immigration. In addition to its relationship to the evolving history of interest in American antiques, the American Wing can be read as a political statement. The remarks made by the museum trustees at the opening of the building confirm such a reading. As Wendy Kaplan has noted in her study of the Wing's principal overseer, R. T. H. Halsey: "The silent objects were transformed into eloquent assertions of American ideals which would remind citizens of the integrity, honesty, and courage of their forefathers and encourage them to emulate their goals."

The American Wing was part of a larger movement in the 1920's to create "shrines" of American democracy. In 1926, Henry Ford established The Edison Institute in the shadow of his automobile plant in Dearborn, Michigan. Ford planned his museum and a country village as a testament to American enterprise and as a recollection of the humble roots from which he and other successful Americans had sprung. Ford hoped through architecture and objects to capture the spirit and energy that had motivated him and other inventors, capitalists, and politicians to the creation of modern America. History was an inspiration and a device for testing modern achievement.

At the other end of the spectrum, another lesson in American history was being written in the streets of a sleepy town in Virginia as John D. Rockefeller, Jr., dedicated the power of his vast resources to the restoration and reconstruction of the colonial capital of Virginia at Williamsburg. Here in bricks and mortar the confrontation between power and the people was celebrated and the triumph of democracy over tyranny was reenacted. In the process, advanced techniques in historic sites archeology were established and the flame was turned up under historical and architectural research, setting new standards for American museums. Williamsburg's focus on the craftsman, his tools and techniques, and the living environment in which objects were used gave greater range and depth to the presentation of American things. The accumulation of the types of European objects that would have been imported for use gave further background to the understanding of style sources.

Because of the individuals involved, these projects in Michigan and Virginia had wide public exposure. The press reported on the collecting and research activities as well as on the record prices of such objects at public sale. The founding of *The Magazine Antiques* in 1922 also indicates the existence of a dedicated and interested community of collectors and a body of authors who could supply articles on antique subjects on a regular basis. The magazine also created an advertising forum that helped expand the market beyond the narrow parameters of the East Coast. It is an interesting sidelight that, so early in the history of collecting American furniture, the prestigious firm of Israel Sack in their first advertisement in *Antiques* emphasized the investment value of American furniture. They were clearly appealing to a new class of collectors beyond the traditionally cultured upper class.

In 1928, the Boston Museum of Fine Arts opened a new decorative arts wing and the Philadelphia Museum of Art inaugurated a new building that included both American and European period rooms. The Brooklyn Museum, which had been collecting American interiors since 1915, opened nineteen early rooms under the direction of Luke Vincent Lockwood. As early as 1902, Lockwood had published the landmark volume *Colonial Furniture in America* and he was influential in assuring the extreme accuracy of the Brooklyn installations. In several instances, an entire floor of a building was resurrected, thus preserving the original disposition of rooms as well as their precise size and shape. Such care was unusual in most installations where rooms had to be adapted to available space.

By the end of the decade all of the necessary components were in place for the broad-based development of interest in American antiques. The marketplace was given a final boost by The First International Antiques Exposition held at the Hotel Commodore in New York City in 1929 and by the Boston Antiques Exhibition staged at the Statler Hotel the same year. In addition to these trade exhibitions, another event of 1929 had a major impact on American collecting—a charitable benefit for the Girl Scouts of America. Over three hundred pieces of American furniture, decorative objects, and glass were borrowed from private collectors and installed at the prestigious Anderson Galleries in New York City. This survey of three centuries of American production and its accompanying catalogue were intended to demonstrate unequivocally the excellence of American design and the sophistication of American craftsmanship. The collection was displayed in roomlike settings arranged by the major lender to the exhibition, Henry Francis du Pont. The Girl Scouts Loan Exhibition was the first extended public showing of what du Pont had been doing in the six years since he had started collecting in the American field.

The attempt to emulate Chinese ceramics led to an orientalizing of such heavier-bodied European earthenwares as the delft posset pot on top of the Japanned high chest in the Cecil Bedroom (above and left). The scrolled flower and vine designs on the crewel-embroidered window and bed hangings suggest other eastern influences. The polychrome crewel embroidery on the bedspread is worked over and around an appliquéd tape that forms a strapwork design. The spread is believed to have been inherited by John Hancock from his uncle Thomas, a stationer and bookseller in Boston during the first half of the eighteenth century

*Style does not move with the clear logic and precise rhythm of a military parade but flows in uneven swells and eddies. The displays at Winterthur illustrate the intersections between styles and regions. Within rooms, smaller displays are clustered to show a variety of forms, such as the Chinese export porcelain in the popular Famille Rose pattern in the Gamon Room (top). A leather-covered chair pulled up to an open desk in the Wentworth Room (opposite) focuses on the fact that fall-front desks were a new form in the eighteenth century. The use of single architec-*

*tural details in corridors and display areas heightens the dialogue between buildings and furniture. The doorway to Massachusetts Hall (above left) comes from Mordington, built about 1785, near Frederica, Delaware. It frames a desk and bookcase that was made between 1785 and 1795 for the flamboyant Boston merchant Joseph Barrell. Exemplary objects lined up in the long hall of the 1928–31 wing (above right) are isolated into groups by a succession of arched openings whose detailing amplifies the ornamental vocabulary of adjacent furniture*

The rooms at Winterthur are organized around a clear domestic function, but the furniture was chosen and positioned for visual and dramatic effect. The period and style of the architecture of the rooms conditioned the choice of furnishings. Many of the rooms came from southern houses, generally of grander scale than their New England counterparts, but relatively little southern furniture survives. While the South has long been thought to have depended on furniture transported from the North or imported from England, imports also played a part in New England inte-riors. Such new forms as the high chest in the Wentworth Room (top) or the daybed in the Walnut Room (opposite top) were originated for the court and its followers and found their way into middle-class circles. The early eighteenth-century furniture of the William and Mary style was of a stately scale and seems to strain at the restrictions of the low-slung and heavily structural shape of the seventeenth-century Wentworth Room in which it is displayed. This setting provides an exciting foil for the rich veneers, graceful spirals, and airy dignity of this baroque-derived style

*Small objects of metal, ceramic, and glass were more easily transported than furniture and not only formed a staple of international commerce but also became the vehicle for the transfer of styles. Imported ceramics from Europe and the Orient range from tin-glazed earthenware, such as the rare Nevers ware in the Wentworth Room, to the continental delft mantel garnitures in the Walnut Room, to the English efforts at duplicating Chinese wares. The Worcester water bottle and bowl in the Port Royal Bedroom (opposite right) mimic the early eighteenth-century*

*Chinese bottle and Japanese bowl (above left). A supplier of raw materials, America also provided a major market for finished wares whose production in the colonies was limited by government regulation. The fireplace equipment in the Essex Room (above right), brass candlesticks, and other lighting devices were imported in huge quantities. Even after the revolution, America depended on such imports as the French clock with the figure of George Washington in the Baltimore Drawing Room (opposite left)*

The eighteenth-century fascination with the rights of man led to revolution in art as well as politics. The neoclassical style, born in the later part of the century, was severe and ordered in contrast to the fanciful arabesques of the rococo style it succeeded. In America, neoclassicism was based on styles of the Greek and Roman democracies and represented a patriotic zeal and the quest for a national identity. An American iconography focused on classical symbols of freedom, republican virtue, and their manifestations in the heroes of the revolution and in native motifs such as the American eagle. Although imported goods flooded the market temporarily and undermined American efforts to establish domestic manufactories, those goods were carried on American ships. This maritime activity led to renewed prosperity of the new nation. In the Franklin Room (top), imported ceramics, cameos, and such pictures as the French engraving after Jean Honoré Fragonard's drawing commemorating the genius of Benjamin Franklin, to the left of the window, all celebrated the role of Franklin as a founding father. America's efforts to compete with imports produced ceramic manufactories, textile mills, and the first domestically manufactured wallpapers. The wallpaper in the Imlay Room (left), recently reproduced, was purchased in 1794 by John Imlay for his house in Allentown, New Jersey, from William Poyntel in Philadelphia, who may well have been its maker. The painted furniture in this room is from Baltimore, which became a center for such fine productions after the revolution and when that city's mercantile role was expanding

In urban areas in America during the eighteenth century, native walnut and then mahogany, the latter imported from Cuba and the West Indies, were the favored woods for the finest furniture. These richly figured and fine-grained woods were ideal for the bold massing and intricate carving of the baroque and rococo styles. Maple and cherry, often associated with rural or simple city furniture, was more colorful and less expensive. The Maple Room (above and top), with woodwork from Port Royal painted in the soft tones favored by du Pont, contains Winterthur's most ambitious, finely worked, and richly grained maple pieces. The rich honey color of the Philadelphia high chest (top) and desk and bookcase (above) is complemented by the bold earth tones of the English Axminster-type hand-knotted carpet. Color became increasingly important in the coordinated decorative schemes of the late eighteenth and nineteenth centuries. Painted furniture, previously reserved for utilitarian purposes, became a fashionable byproduct of neoclassicism. Gilt decoration of musical or military trophies emulated costlier cast ormolu mounts or fine inlays found on natural-grained furniture

111

In the early eigtheenth century, styles were named for ruling monarchs. With the rise of Englishmen Thomas Chippendale as a furniture maker and publicist, Robert Adam as an architect and interior designer, and George Hepplewhite and Thomas Sheraton as popularizers, more frequent and rapid changes of taste emerged, and styles were named for their designers. The upholsterer, too, became a critical figure. The gold silk taffeta workbag is a perfect counterpoint to the exotic woods—satinwood, rosewood, and ebony—of this Philadelphia kidney-shaped worktable in the McIntire Room (above). A stylish container for a woman's handwork, the worktable also suggests the increasing importance of women's decisions in taste and decorating. The swag carving on the post of the mahogany Philadelphia bed is an example of neoclassical design. The oil lamp emphasizes the role of light in performing domestic functions and the rapid improvements that would be made in lighting during the nineteenth century, altering completely the organization of furniture in a room since the window was no longer the primary source of light

# A COLLECTOR EMERGES

Henry Francis du Pont had moved into his father's house when he returned to Winterthur from college in 1902. It is unlikely that a man who in all aspects of his life expressed subtle aesthetic judgments would have been oblivious to his surroundings inside the house but he was living in the home of his father, who was equally strong willed. While Henry Francis exercised control over the planning of the gardens and grounds, he probably had little to say about the interior arrangements. Indeed, there may have been a subtle loathing for the sham renaissance and classical styles of decoration used in the new wing of the house. He certainly had no use for the furniture of his childhood home and remarked later, "As my only acquaintance with American mahogany was with the Empire veneered variety which had been in the home of my family and which I heartily disliked, I decided we would not have a piece of it...." When he furnished his own apartment after his marriage he filled it with English and French antiques. It was not until the 1920's that he discovered American furnishings.

It is no surprise that, in light of his two decades of gardening activity, when he first "saw" American furniture in 1923 it was a color harmony that attracted him. While on a visit to Mrs. J. Watson Webb, the daughter of Impressionist painting collectors Mr. and Mrs. Horace O. Havemeyer, at her Shelburne, Vermont, home, he was "fascinated by the colors of a pine dresser filled with pink Staffordshire plates." His previous familiarity with American antiques is uncertain. Scattered through the family houses along the Brandywine were numerous examples of early furniture that descended through generations of the family. In later

years, in fact, he proudly displayed many of these pieces and other family-related objects he was able to acquire for Winterthur. His frequent trips to see his sister in New England would also have provided opportunities to see fine American furniture. As an avid visitor to museums, especially after settling into his New York City apartment, he would have been able to see the American objects that were on view. Museum visits did influence him, he recalled: "Repeated trips to many museums gave me endless pleasure as well as training in colors and proportion, and seeing many French and English houses was a liberal education in period interiors." Often he was less inspired by individual objects than by their ensemble. Concerning his visit to Mrs. Webb's, he noted that it "gave me...my first introduction to an early-American interior." At this stage it was not high-style furniture of dark hardwood but the buttery softness and homespun air of simpler forms, often in light-toned fruitwoods.

In one of those rare coincidences that irrevocably change an individual, within a few days of seeing the Webb pine dresser he found himself at Beauport, on Eastern Point in Gloucester, Massachusetts. There the small light that had flickered in Shelburne turned into an inspiring flame. Beauport, now the property of the Society for the Preservation of New England Antiquities, was begun in 1907 by Henry Davis Sleeper, a Boston-born architect and decorator trained in the beaux-arts tradition. In his own house on a rocky neck opposite Gloucester, he created a picturesque and rambling structure fitted with architectural details and paneling from early American houses. Sleeper's use of antiques was more imaginative than accurate in their organization and display. His taste led

*Pine kitchen (top) at Beauport, Gloucester, Massachusetts, the home of Henry Davis Sleeper, who influenced du Pont in his early collecting. Sleeper supplied antiques and helped arrange the rooms at Chestertown House (above), du Pont's "American" house built in Southampton, Long Island. This southeastern view of the house was taken in 1969*

toward light-colored furniture contrasted with dark walls and accented by concentrated displays of such accessories as tole, pewter, glass, and ceramics. Sleeper painted with a broad brush and coordinated light and spatial sequences that were by turn charming or dramatic. He found in early objects the raw material for innovative decorative schemes; objects were chosen and massed for color, texture, and shape. Hooked rugs with strong geometric and floral patterns enlivened the rooms and odd angles and low-pitched ceilings emphasized hominess and enclosure. Domesticity was announced by a fully furnished pine kitchen and reiterated by ruffled curtains and bedhangings. His use of light—either sunlight modified by displays of colored glass in the windows or through the extensive use of fixtures—was beguiling, and du Pont later wrote him: "I find your lights are so delightfully arranged—so cleverly placed with always some definite effect in mind—that it makes me quite desperate about my perfectly conventional arrangements of lights, and I wonder if you could take the time to look over my plans and suggest some other places for outlets, which might or might not be used as we required."

The total effect of Beauport was an inspiration, enchanting and intimate, and totally at odds with the baronial atmosphere of Winterthur at that time. Sleeper's house would have been a revelation for anyone unfamiliar with the decorative possibilities of American objects. For du Pont it was a challenge: he was determined to create "an American house." Thinking of his apartment in New York, the house in Delaware, and the countless homes he had visited, he told his wife: "Everybody has English houses and half the furniture I know... is new. Since we're Americans it's much more interesting to have American furniture." He saw an arena for creativity and felt as challenged as he would have been had he been laying out a new garden or making further innovations in his breeding program.

Henry Francis du Pont was forty-three years old when he began collecting American antiques. It is intriguing to speculate what changes he had in mind for the day when Winterthur was to become his. His father was eighty-five and his sister was happily settled in New England. She had just acquired the original du Pont house, Eleutherian Mills. The mills along the Brandywine River were abandoned in 1920 and the company-owned houses near the powder yards were sold to family members. Louise was at that moment contemplating the restoration of the house that she would furnish with antiques. Her brother admonished her to preserve the remnants of the old mills as "historic remains." Du Pont was close to his sister and shared enthusiasms and interests. Her opinions influenced his collecting activities, and he often discussed his discoveries with her. In her own right she was well known in her field and made important contributions to the historic preservation movement in America. Du Pont must surely have received support and encouragement from his sister in the planning of his American house.

When Henry Francis began building his American house at a seaside location in Southampton, Long Island, he asked Sleeper to help him with the architecture of the rooms, color, textiles, and lights. Sleeper would have had ready access to supply houses and would have been familiar with the problems of installing architectural details removed from other locations. Most of the surviving correspondence between them is con-

cerned with accessories rather than with major objects. In that area, du Pont was on his own and appears to have acted with unaccustomed haste.

According to an oft-repeated story, the first piece of American furniture he acquired came shortly after he decided to build his American home. By his own account, one Sunday, instead of going to church, he went antiquing. A few miles from Winterthur, in Media, Pennsylvania, he spied and bought a Pennsylvania walnut chest with the date 1737 inlaid on the top drawer. In addition to the chest, he acquired "some Philadelphia woodwork," from the same dealer, H. L. Lindsey. In fact, these were not the first American antiques du Pont acquired. As early as 1919, he had bought a maple table from an auction at the American Art Association in New York and during the following years he bought a number of pieces of early American glass. In late 1922 and early 1923, he made additional purchases of glass and several pieces of maple furniture at auctions at the Anderson Galleries. On October 10, 1923, he bought a walnut high case, a few days before his "first purchase." While he may have considered the maple furniture insignificant and not worth serious consideration as antiques, his faulty recollection is more interesting than a mere lapse of memory after a thirty-year career of intensive collecting. The Lindsey purchases represented for du Pont a clear example of his collecting biases. The choice of a dated piece of furniture was characteristic of a desire for documentation and authority that was to become a dominant collecting trait. Among the Philadelphia woodwork was a mantel embellished with a scene of the battle of Lake Erie. In subsequent purchases du Pont showed a marked preference for objects with historical meaning or symbolic imagery. The fact that he bought architectural details at the same time that he bought furniture also indicates the direction his installations would take. In addition, on the same day, he bought a slant-top desk, a candlestand, and a pair of blown candy jars from Lindsey; in the ensuing two-and-a-half months he bought nearly one hundred pieces of furniture, many from dealers in the immediate vicinity of Winterthur.

During the following year his antiques purchases numbered more than seven hundred and in 1925 he added more than twelve hundred objects. His purchases in subsequent years continued unabated. He also continued buying architectural details and entire rooms of paneling through local dealers. As several of the rooms came from houses in Chestertown, Maryland, he decided to name his new home on Long Island Chestertown House. According to du Pont, once the woodwork was assembled, he hired the architect John W. Cross "to draw me plans for a house to incorporate them, keeping the original sizes and placing of windows and doors of the rooms. When Chestertown House...was finished, I equipped it with early furniture, some much earlier than the house, which was in the style of about 1770." Rejecting the mahogany furniture that he had disliked from childhood and which was probably too dark and formal for a seaside house, he chose "pine, walnut, fruit, and other native woods."

Du Pont was instinctively concerned with accuracy of detail and the integrity of his settings. He preferred to keep the Chestertown rooms as close to the original as possible and asked his architect to design the house around them. The approach was quite different from Sleeper's,

where a theatrical organization of space was the ideal. On occasion, du Pont was obliged to alter the original design of a room by moving doors and windows or using paneling as sheathing in rooms whose modern scale was inconsistent with period examples. He also used architectural fragments in isolation for decorative effect. While his choice of light woods may have been a rejection of his childhood surroundings, it was also clearly an echo of Sleeper's decorating preferences; in fact, many of his mentor's ideas were absorbed by du Pont and introduced into Chestertown House. Du Pont's purchases in these years had much of the same homespun quality that characterized the furnishings of Beauport. In addition to furniture, he bought heavily in American glass and English Staffordshire wares, quilts, tinware, Pennsylvania German objects and hooked rugs. In the last months of 1923, during his first surge of buying, he also bought a blue and white slipcover, a pair of hinges, a burl bowl, an iron foot scraper, rush bottom chairs, a fire lighter, a beehive, and a spinning wheel among other purchases.

It is hard to judge the exact appearance of Chestertown House from surviving photographs as furniture and architectural details were removed over the years and incorporated into Winterthur. Judging by the volume of purchases, it was heavily furnished. In a letter written to Thomas T. Waterman in 1933, du Pont suggests that the process of removing objects to Winterthur was already far advanced within a decade of the completion of Chestertown House: "I thought one time of having an elaborate catalogue made of that house and had even begun it, but when I discovered that there were about three times as many articles there as in

the Metropolitan Museum and that it took all sorts of different people to write a catalogue, I decided to bring the best things back from there to here [Winterthur] and eventually include them in the write-up of this house which sooner or later will have to be done." This letter also contains the tantalizing implication that even this early du Pont envisioned Winterthur as a museum. In fact, as early as 1927 he had written to Sleeper asking, "Could you give me some idea of the manner in which Mrs. Jack Gardner's house in Boston was left as a museum? And what provision was made in her will in this respect, if the house was left in trust? Or did she create a company with the trustees as directors? What provision was made for its maintenance and what restrictions are there?... I am thinking of doing something of the kind with the Southampton house—not that I think that it is in a class with Fenway Court." The Winterthur Corporation, a nonprofit educational foundation, was established on February 25, 1930.

House museums were a relatively new phenomenon at this time. Although the focus of early preservation activities had been on houses generally associated with early historic figures, the development of such attractions had been slow. The general expansion of interest in the American historical past during the 1920's, reflected in such activities as the founding of the American Wing and the creation of Greenfield Village and Colonial Williamsburg, had a more localized manifestation in the opening of restored and furnished historic houses in many small communities. The number of such houses grew from ten in 1895 to more than four hundred in 1930. Improved roads and greater numbers of automo-

*Stereopticon views taken at Winterthur in May 1935 show the Pine Kitchen (opposite) and Pine Hall (left). Both these rooms, with their concentrations of rural furniture and strongly patterned hooked rugs, recall the interiors of Chestertown House. They have now been replaced by the Kershner Parlor and Kitchen*

biles provided the mobility that made such activities practical and desirable. It is therefore not surprising that du Pont may have been thinking of creating a museum out of his house. In 1930, he drew up an extensive plan for the conversion of Chestertown House into a museum after his death, and in a fascinating twenty-three-page document spelled out the exact form and organization of such a museum "to afford all those interested an opportunity to view and to study the conditions surrounding the early American home life." At the same time, visitors were to be treated to a glimpse of Henry Francis du Pont's home life, as the house was to be maintained largely as it was during his occupation. He detailed the exact location of the furniture as well as the creation of new display areas in old servants' rooms. He described what flowers and plants should be put on which table and how the house and contents were to be maintained. Color was a major concern, and he instructed his trustees to preserve the wall colors unless replacement fabrics were required, in which case the wall colors could be adjusted appropriately. The curator was to "take a personal interest in the appearance of the house. The locations of most of the contents of the house are now indicated on blueprints," he noted, "but it often takes a push here and a poke there to make things look right. The Curator, therefore, should be chosen for his ability as a decorator as well as for any other qualification. No blueprint or servant in the world will ever get things looking the way they should, and it takes a personal touch—an inch here and an inch there in any special arrangement makes all the difference."

An inch here and there was about as much latitude as anyone was

granted. Chestertown House had been documented in photography and a full catalogue was to be issued. Certain additional rooms and display areas were to be created out of servants' rooms and service spaces and furnished with objects brought from Winterthur, even though he "might possibly leave that as a Museum of furniture, etc." Du Pont clearly wished to leave the museum as a document of his taste and judgment and wanted to keep it in a way that would "retain its charm." If the trustees introduced objects other than those specified by him or allowed any rearrangement of the furnishings, the ownership of the property was to pass to the University of Delaware and the contents sold to raise professorial salaries and sustain scholarships.

At heart, then, there was an educational motive; this is reflected also in his scheme for interpreting the collections. Chestertown House was to be shown to small groups of visitors, generally no more than three or four in a party. There were to be no "classes of young children, or any classes from a young ladies' school or seminary," but rather fee-paying adults who would bring a mature and open mind to the experience. Clearly du Pont was remembering the hordes of people rushed through European houses and museums and wanted no such sideshow atmosphere. With small groups, there was no need for barricades or cases which remove visitors from the direct experience of the place. He further instructed: "The men guards or women guards are to be suitably dressed, clean and neat, and not look at visitors as if they are robbers or have no business there. Their attitude should be more that of a librarian or well-trained servant, helpful but not intruding in any way." The guides were not to have a me-

*Chestertown Room, from a house built in Chestertown, Maryland, c. 1762. The handsome architecture of this room helped move du Pont toward the collecting of more sophisticated American antiques than those installed in his Long Island house*

120

morized speech but should let the thoughtful visitor look and be available to answer questions when asked. He felt that groups of more than four would splinter into smaller clusters and engage in side conversations having nothing to do with what they were looking at. Accustomed as he was to thoughtful observation, he wanted others to do the same. In this 1930 document, he spelled out many of the principles and conditions that would apply to the founding of the Henry Francis du Pont Winterthur Museum two decades later. He also took the first step toward that goal in the same year with the creation of the Winterthur Corporation as a charitable and educational foundation.

Such a didactic purpose is also hinted at in one of du Pont's accounts of the founding of his collections at Winterthur. "I came in contact with widely divergent early American materials of all kinds. The problem of giving them appropriate recognition inevitably came to my mind. After the opening of the 'American Wing' at the Metropolitan Museum in New York in 1924, and another such wing in the Brooklyn Museum…it occurred to me to undertake a similar venture, and I decided to add an American Wing to Winterthur, which I had inherited at about this time."

Within five years of the beginnings of his serious collecting he was not simply furnishing a house but creating a museum. The conversion to this larger purpose may have come about as a result of inheriting the vast estate at Winterthur and the challenge that its maintenance posed. If the challenge had enlarged, so had his range of collecting. Vast new fields of interest were emerging for him as he was caught up in the intoxicating sport that had become his main occupation. In his published reminiscence he offered a more compact explanation of his shift in collecting focus:

> When Chestertown House was almost finished I had occasion to buy another paneled room from Chestertown. I realized it was too sophisticated for the other rooms in the Southampton house; so for the time being I stored it in my barn in Delaware. As time went on, I developed the plan of adding this and other rooms to Winterthur, my family home near Wilmington, in order to create a wing that would show America as it had been. Through friends, I learned of Belle Isle house at Boer, Virginia; the Port Royal house near Frankford Junction, Pennsylvania; Readbourne in Maryland; and other eighteenth-century houses from which I was able to acquire much of the original woodwork.

Henry Francis du Pont's father had died late in 1926 and early the following year Henry Francis inherited Winterthur. Within a year he had woodwork from Chestertown and Centerville, Maryland; he had rooms from Tappahannock, in Virginia; from the Pickering House in North East, Maryland; and Belle Isle in storage and had measured drawings of these rooms on hand. In the case of Belle Isle, a mid-eighteenth-century house, he had acquired most of the components of the house including a parlor, small hall, living room, hall, ceiling, stairs, second floor hall, dining room, bedroom, and kitchen. Du Pont was following an already-established custom in removing extensive interior woodwork from early houses. He appears to have been conscientious in his acquisitions and withdrew in the face of local preservation efforts. But the spirit and adventure of restoring old houses had not yet infected America despite the enthusiasm for colonial architectural styles in new residential construction. Many of the buildings from which Winterthur and other museum interiors came would have perished from neglect leaving no physical evidence of their existence. It is possible that these museum installations helped develop the taste for early interiors that subsequently led to the development of a broad-based preservation movement in America.

The account of the acquisition of Port Royal in February 1928 includes the characteristic description of the decayed condition in which many early houses were discovered. The house was found by J. A. Lloyd Hyde, a young antiques dealer and friend of du Pont who was not only responsible for supplying some of the finest decorative accessories for Winterthur but also was du Pont's nominee in 1930 to be curator of Chestertown House. Hyde reminisced about Port Royal: "I used to go past this rather derelict Georgian house on the train, it wasn't very far off. So eventually I took the elevated railway out from Philadelphia and walked to it from the last station at the end of the line. I found that it was a Polish club. It was in the most miserable neighborhood, sort of factories." Removing the interior details was not always easy. In an effort to rescue the decorated plaster ceiling at Port Royal, the joists had to be cut from the room above and the ceiling lowered intact from above. Du Pont had the advantage of a hard-working and well-equipped crew available from the ranks of his farm and estate workers and he came to rely increasingly on his own staff for the accurate documentation of woodwork before its removal.

In May 1928, du Pont asked Wilmington architect Albert Ely Ives to begin working on a month-to-month retainer to prepare plans for a large addition to Winterthur that would, in fact, more than double the size of the existing structure. In his letter to Ives he noted, "Should the plans be accepted, I shall have Miss Marian Coffin as the landscape architect for the outside work, etc., and Henry Sleeper probably will have charge of the interior decorating." The choice of Marian Coffin was logical and appropriate; together she and du Pont would evolve a handsome integration of house and landscape.

Sleeper's selection was more nettlesome. In the five years since the commencement of Chestertown House, du Pont had matured considerably. Sleeper himself recognized this and wrote to du Pont, albeit flatteringly, "I always think of you as one of my clients who has just as much energy and imagination in these matters as I have. I am pleased and flattered when you want my help, but between ourselves I think you are about as capable as I am." In fact, Sleeper no longer had the energy and enthusiasm for such an undertaking and his relationship with du Pont ended just short of acrimony.

Du Pont had grown beyond Sleeper and had become an original thinker working in the high style idiom that he had come to not only because the more elegant woodwork he had bought demanded it, but because these forms offered a new collecting challenge. "Chippendale furniture... appealed to me," du Pont wrote, because, "It was sturdy, and suitable for practical use. Also, I was interested in its many variations, not only within one type, such as Philadelphia chairs, but among the widely dif-

fering products of regions showing different influences—Boston, Newport, New York, and Philadelphia."

As his father had before, du Pont decided to preserve the existing structure at Winterthur, including the tiny block surviving from the first residence, adding a long wing to its southern face. The planning of the "American Wing" at Winterthur was an ambitious and well-organized project. The structure was to house "period" rooms, which like those at Southampton were to be lived in. Their disposition at Winterthur was formal and consistent with the elaborateness of life there. A new entrance to the house was centered in the long western facade of the wing; the old en-

*High chest from Boston, 1740–50. Made by John Pimm. White pine, hard and soft maple, with Japanned decoration. Height: 95¾"*

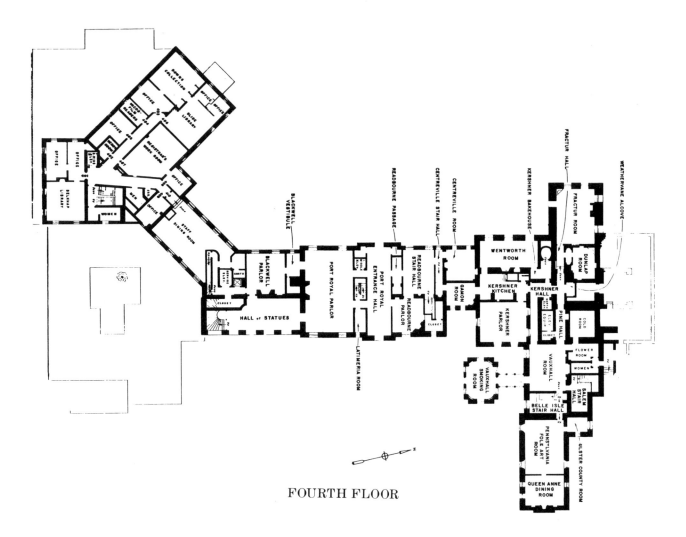

FOURTH FLOOR

try on the north face was covered with a conservatory. The earlier portions of the house were stripped of their 1902 ornaments and simplified to bring them in harmony with the design of the new wing. Elaborate window surrounds, balconies, and dormers were either eliminated or altered and the textured tile roof replaced with plain tiles. New dormers based on designs from Port Royal were added. It was also from Port Royal that the entrance pavilion details, as well as the wide entrance hall and grand reception room, were taken. The handsome architectural elaboration of this mid-Georgian structure influenced the design of adjacent spaces.

In addition to exterior detailing, the design of the wing posed numerous problems for both architect and patron. Creating a large structure that would fit comfortably into its hillside location and join older portions of the house without overpowering them was a clear concern. The task of introducing sufficient light into the small period interiors and coordinating the fenestration of varying-sized rooms on the facades also taxed the designer's skill. His solution was to create a long narrow wing that connected the southern facade of the old house in the center of what had been the original Winterthur house. Rooms in this wing were arranged contiguously, paralleling a central hall that bisected the wing and connected it with the older house. All the rooms had an outside wall permitting windows that faced the surrounding lawns and gardens. Despite the colonial details of the rooms, the windows were designed to be consistent with those in the older wing and were in the form of French casements rather than the mullioned sash type that would have been appropriate in a colonial interior. This decision was made not only for consistency but also because

*Plans of Winterthur, 1928–45. The long axis runs in a north-south direction. Because of the hillside location, the fourth floor became the entrance level for the 1928–31 wing, which is separated from the older portions of the house by the Gamon Room.*

124

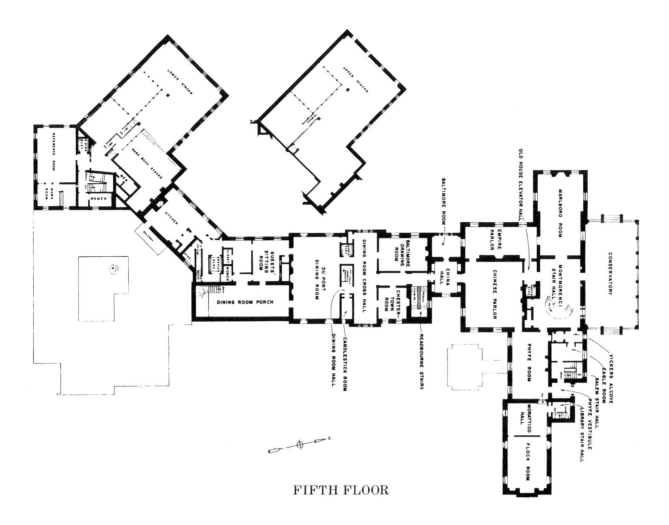

FIFTH FLOOR

du Pont felt the French windows allowed more air and light into the rooms. He would come to regret this decision and later replaced them with more appropriate windows.

The new wing created a T-shaped plan with the old house. At the foot of the wing, a secondary service wing angled to the southwest, creating an arm that mirrored the northern section and producing a modified U shape on the entrance facade and a gentle embrace for arriving guests. The angle of the service wing also allowed more light for the dining room porch and the upper garden terrace that would otherwise have been cast into deep shadow because of the exaggerated extent and height of the wing.

The modesty of detailing on the western facade stemmed in part from the necessity of coordinating so many windows for the many small rooms on the interior. It also grew out of a traditional architectural concept that the facade should express dignity and reserve in contrast with the more playful approach permitted on the garden front.

The house was really an envelope for the interiors and an incident in the landscape. It was not meant to express strong personality or impress in the way a great urban mansion or a typical country estate might. It was concealed as much as possible within the surrounding woodlands. The close environment had made the quantity of windows all the more necessary. Du Pont was as concerned as his father had been with preserving the woody surroundings. Construction photographs reveal how the wing was wedged into the woody hillside. Prized plantings received special attention. After examining the plans for the new wing du Pont wrote the ar-

*The Pine Kitchen and Wentworth Room on the fourth floor and the Chinese and Empire parlors on this floor occupy the space of the 1839 Winterthur house. To the left of that block is the wing added in 1902 by Henry Algernon du Pont*

125

chitect that he would probably need to move basement hot water pipes as he felt they might be too close to the roots of a favored wisteria and kill the plant. He then chided the architect to make other necessary provisions for the beloved vine: "Show the exact place on the new house you wish the wisteria to be placed, as naturally we will have to have enormous iron hooks built into the house while under construction to hold it up and keep it in place. I should like it eventually to reach the railing of my upstairs porch. If you think it is going to disfigure the house to have it go across that way, I will have to plant a new vine and have me dead before it even gets up there." Du Pont had his own construction shed built on the construction site and there, with a set of plans, he would oversee the daily progress. With the extensive reworking of the exterior of the older fabric and the complete gutting of the original house, it was necessary for the family to move out. They established themselves temporarily in a small farm cottage at the foot of the hill on the edge of Clenny Run.

Du Pont watched the progress of the design and construction from a distance as well as from close range. While summering in Southampton during the initial design stage he reviewed the architect's plans and wrote long and detailed letters suggesting problems for the architect's consideration. In one typical eight-page, single-spaced, typed letter written on September 18, 1928, he questioned Ives on such issues as how air would get into the attic, what would happen to the light well in the old house if a new roof garden were constructed and how light would get to the interior rooms of that block, how the elevator mechanic would get to the machinery for repairs, why gutters were not shown on the design, even where the but-

*View of the roof during the construction of the 1928–31 wing. The service areas occupied the block that angles to the right (southwest)*

126

ler would put his ginger ale bottles. He asked about the thickness of the outside walls, whether dormers were exact copies of Port Royal, where the overhead pipes in the old part of the house would go when the kitchen became the pine room, where coal would be kept should they decide to install a coal range, and if there would be a door to bring wood into the house since the front door could only be used when they were not in residence. The smooth workings of this grand machine for living were of equal concern to the aesthetic issues. Future alterations and needs were also anticipated. In one instance he requested that pipes be installed in case he wanted to put a bathroom in a certain area sometime in the future.

Du Pont's concern for detail throughout the three-year campaign was unflagging. A typical example of his discussion concerning lockers for the golf room: "I shall naturally want very up-to-date lockers—that is, I want them somewhat larger than the average locker, as each locker must hold a set of golf clubs and bag as well as a tennis racquet. They are also to have a shelf to hold one pair of shoes, and probably a shelf for a hat or something of the kind." As this small room was on the first floor of the north side of the house, the ceilings were extremely high. Even the space above the lockers did not escape his attention: "I am thinking of exhibiting above the golf lockers my collection of costumes, etc., which I got in the Near East some twenty years ago. I might do two things—I might get several dummy figures and dress them up in these clothes, or I might simply have the costumes hanging in cabinets. In either case they will have to be under glass, as it is too much like work keeping those things clean all the time." This letter, which constituted a major design review, was written five months after the architect began planning the building. As du Pont gave the go-ahead to proceed to the next stage, he underscored his dual concern with aesthetics and practicality. "I think all the facades look very well," he wrote encouragingly, "and if we are not sacrificing too many practical things and can get the outside fixed up so that we can get in and out of the house without having to use ladders and what not, I think we may almost start to finish the plans in order to get the estimates. I shudder to think of having to place electric lights, telephones, push buttons, etc." Ever mindful of the gardens, he added a postscript, "Have you sent the blueprints to Miss Coffin's office yet? If not, for God's sake hurry and do it at once."

Marian Cruger Coffin's design for the terraced gardens would integrate the house with its surroundings. From an ornamental point of view the garden facade was the more interesting side of the house. The plain western facade, although providing the entrance, faced an old farm house and looked toward woodlands. This practical prospect was screened by the dense plantings immediately next to the house, while the northern and eastern fronts looked out upon the woodland gardens and across the low valley to the southeast with its rolling meadows and bucolic scenery.

The reciprocal view of the house from garden and fields was a lively and varied silhouette, an American house masquerading as a French chateau. The principal American features of the northern and eastern fronts were the monumental columns that framed the conservatory and the two-story open porch off the dining room. Du Pont had carefully scanned Fiske Kimball's *Domestic Architecture of the American Colonies and of*

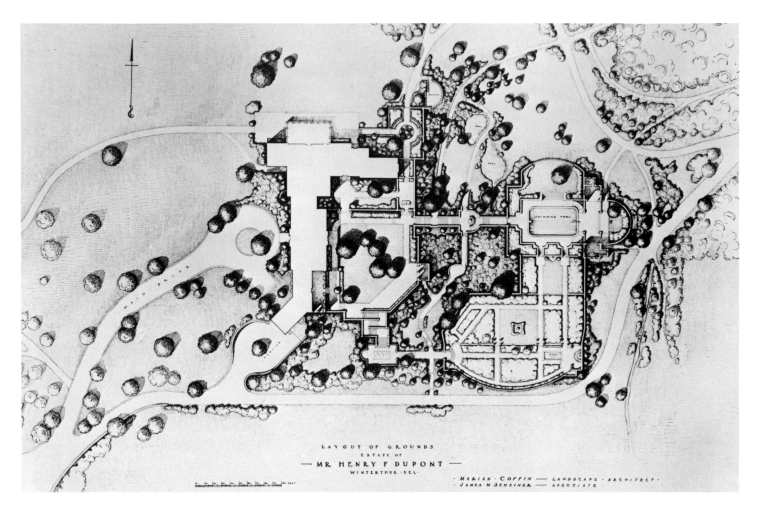

LAYOUT OF GROUNDS
ESTATE OF
— MR. HENRY F DUPONT —
WINTERTHUR · DEL·

· MARIAN · COFFIN —— LANDSCAPE · ARCHITECT ·
· JAMES M SCHEINER —— ASSOCIATE ·

*the Early Republic* and Coffin and Holden's *Brick Architecture of the Colonial Period in Maryland and Virginia* in search of precedents and recommended numerous plates in these volumes to the architect. The ultimate prototypes for these monumental orders came from a nearby Philadelphia country seat, the Woodlands, built in 1788 for William Hamilton. The ionic pilasters on the north front of that house served as the model for the pilasters of Winterthur's conservatory, while the giant Tuscan order on the south front of the Woodlands was adapted for the columns, entablature, and pilasters of the Winterthur porch.

This bookish concern with prototypes lends credence to the comment du Pont would subsequently make to Sleeper that he was doing the house "archeologically and correctly" but the size of the building demanded imagination as well as precedent. That imagination is best seen in the garden front. The embrace of the intersecting wings was deeper on this side than on the west and a spirited array of porches, loggia, pavilions, and picturesque roof lines accentuated by tall chimneys provided a series of rich embellishments. The spirit of variety and contrast was echoed in the adjacent gardens, and through a clever arrangement of terrace levels, Marian Coffin concealed the elevated position of the entrance level that was actually on the fourth floor of the house. The steeply sloping hillside was transformed into a high terrace level with commanding views of the gardens and valley below. It was encircled by a balustrade and focused on a stone gazebo that counterpointed the looming mass of the house. The terrace was largely lawn but also featured several monumental poplars reaching to the upper stories of the house. These, like all ancient speci-

mens, were carefully retained. In later years, when one of these trees was choked with the euonymus that would ultimately kill it, du Pont is reported to have remarked, "Six months after I go that tree can be cut down, but not until then." The tree died before the long-lived du Pont and he would not allow it to be cut down while he was in residence. According to John Sweeney, "Du Pont said that while he was in Florida it could be cut down. But he couldn't bear to have that tree cut while he was anywhere around. It was right outside his sitting room."

Stairways descended from the terrace to garden levels below. Immediately to the east, a steep flight enshrouded in enormous boxwoods descended past a sundial to a swimming pool created out of the old garden pool. This sun-dappled area was ornamented with two stone pool houses recalling the gazebo of the upper terrace, and was tied to the adjacent gardens through a rockwork garden and waterfalls created by Coffin along its northern boundaries. Below, a more formal prospect of steep terraces with herbaceous borders led to a rose garden on the lowest level. This garden was also reached from the upper terrace by a grand staircase on its southern edge that descended in ramps, which were frequently filled with potted flowering plants. The Edenic tranquillity of the ensemble remains a strong memory even after new museum buildings replaced many of these features.

The plan of the 1928–31 wing was organized around a suite of entertaining and reception rooms. The entrance crossed the axis of the long central hall and on the first floor of the new wing the plan simulated a typical colonial central hall house plan. The central hall from Port Royal was

*Plan of the grounds at Winterthur (opposite) by Marian Cruger Coffin, showing the terraced gardens to the east of the house. Winterthur from the southeast (above) as it appeared from 1931 to 1946*

widened and lengthened to span the entire width of the wing, and opened directly onto the upper garden terrace. On the south side of the entrance hall a formal parlor from Port Royal was similarly enlarged to provide a grand reception room furnished with some of the most spectacular pieces of Philadelphia Chippendale furniture in the collection. To the north side of the entrance hall two rooms from Readbourne in Maryland were constructed, providing a smaller sitting room and a hall with stairs to the upper levels of the house. Because of the extreme height of these rooms and their hillside location their floor level was below that of the adjacent block of the old house. The upper floors of both sections of the house were of similar height and the break between the two sections was not evident. On the entrance level the connecting link housed a smoking room leading directly to a pine kitchen, created out of the basement kitchen of the old family house and possibly the most visible evidence of Sleeper's influence. This room and the other more informal spaces in the lower levels of the new wing, including the Dancing and Ping-pong rooms, most clearly recalled the colorful homespun approach of Sleeper and were replete with painted and decorated country furniture such as Windsor chairs, settles, dressers, and cupboards often filled with brightly colored and patterned china, treen ware, and decorated tole, hooked rugs, eagle carvings, and architectural fragments.

Next to the Pine Kitchen was the earliest room in the Winterthur ensemble, a room from the seventeenth-century Wentworth House in Portsmouth, New Hampshire, which had been embellished with paneling on the fireplace wall around 1710. As a typical low-ceiling seventeenth-century interior, it provided a perfect setting for the du Ponts' early furniture and fit comfortably into the space reclaimed from the southwestern corner of the basement of the early Winterthur house.

The original block of the Winterthur house was gutted and reworked as a part of the new wing while the 1902 addition was, for the moment, left intact. On the floor above the Port Royal entrance level a huge single room was created to provide a transition between the marble stair hall and the simpler colonial detailing of the wing. The room had the nearly perfect size to house an unusual and brilliant set of Chinese eighteenth-century hand-painted wallpaper. The long hall of the wing led from this room past the morning and breakfast rooms to a cross hall and the dining room. These latter spaces mirrored the entrance hall and parlor below and completed the suite of major public rooms in the new wing. These spaces as well as a multitude of bedrooms, dressing rooms, and hallways on the upper two floors of the wing were fitted out with period woodwork, all of which was planned and installed as a part of the construction of the wing. Although the wing was designed as a shell to accommodate this woodwork, period window and door locations often had to be altered to allow for a plausible sequence within the house, especially in the case of smaller chambers used as bedrooms on the upper floors. Nonetheless, the rooms were considered to be aesthetic and historic entities, not simply sheathing for modern interiors.

The rooms at Winterthur were principally from southern houses. Such interiors, generally larger than northern rooms, tended to be more readily available. Manor and plantation houses from isolated rural areas

were not as carefully guarded and cherished as similar antique structures in the North. Although there was trade and cultural exchange among the colonies, the South was tied more closely to England during the colonial period than the more diversified northern urban economy. Southern architecture was more directly influenced by higher-style design ideas from England as the plantation economy depended on direct commerce with the mother country. Du Pont also probably favored southern interiors because the scale and elegance was in accord with the visions he had for Winterthur. Even the Port Royal rooms, although commodious by any standard, were enlarged to fit the grand design.

In the secondary rooms and in those where totally modern functions prescribed a scale of proportion unfamiliar in an earlier period, the woodwork was adapted. The Ping-pong Room and Dancing Room as well as the Pine Kitchen were treated as settings for objects and although no photographs show the Bowling Alley, it is likely that that area, like the adjacent Badminton Court, had an early American flavor.

These rooms, along with the already existing Billiard Room and Squash Court in the 1902 wing, provided Winterthur with all the recreational amenities of the best country houses. The house had motion picture facilities, and a complete music system was ultimately installed with hidden speakers not only in the house but also in the garden and pool areas. For the comfort of the guests and to maintain sixty or so rooms, a complex range of service and servants' rooms was created. In addition to kitchens, pantries, flower refrigerators, wine cellars, wood storage rooms, and chambermaids' closets, there were china closets, sewing and pressing rooms for

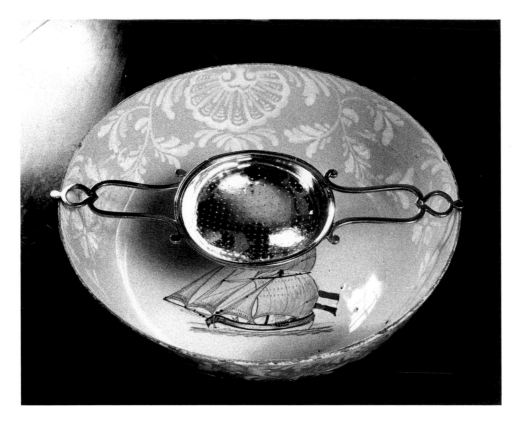

*Polychrome tin-glazed earthen-ware delft bowl (left) from Bristol, England, 1765–75, with an American silver strainer made by Samuel Edwards in Boston, 1735–60. The Baltimore Drawing Room (opposite). The mantel, with plaster composition ornament by Robert Wellford, Philadelphia, c. 1813, was acquired by du Pont in 1923 along with a 1737 chest that was long described as his first American antique purchase. On the table in the foreground is an important silver service by Joseph Richardson, Jr., of Philadelphia*

both housemaids and visiting maids. The butler, secretary, and valet each had a bedroom and a sitting room. In addition to two dozen servants' bedrooms, there were a sitting and dining room for servants. There was even a room dedicated to ice cream. Separate coat closets for house guests and dinner guests suggest the degree of specialized functioning in a house of this scale, a formality that had already disappeared from the English country houses that served as the model for American counterparts. Combined with the gardens and farm staff, the working population of Winterthur at one point reached nearly two hundred fifty people, and the property boasted a ten-hole golf course, tennis courts, its own post office, railroad station, blacksmith, carpenter and butcher shops, and a laundry. Scattered through old farm buildings and new structures were housing for married and unmarried employees and a clubhouse with a theater. A farm band and baseball team all became a part of life at Winterthur. Farm and garden activities continued year round but the house was principally an autumn and spring residence. Summers at Southampton, winters at Boca Grande, Florida, as well as an apartment in New York all took the du Ponts away from Winterthur for long periods of time. But when the house was in full use, for an occasional guest or a large party invited for a country house weekend, the property was alive with activity. The rooms were filled with flowers and the table loaded with comestibles from the farm and gardens. The quality and scale of entertaining is legendary decades after the house ceased to be a home. For Henry Francis du Pont, the favorite house party guest or overnight visitor was one with a dedicated interest in American antiques.

# AMERICAN ANTIQUES IN AN AMERICAN HOUSE

**T**he construction of the new wing at Winterthur took three years. By the time it was completed in 1932, America had suffered an economic collapse and the implications of the depression had become widely felt. It is difficult to determine exactly how the planning and completion of the Winterthur expansion was affected by economic hard times. Financial pressures brought many objects important and otherwise into the marketplace at the same time that the number of buyers was drastically reduced. By the early 1930's Henry du Pont had emerged as a major collector and he was inundated with offers of objects from individuals and from dealers. He had been actively collecting since 1923 and although his activities were initially concentrated on objects that seemed appropriate for Chestertown House, it is likely that he expanded the range of interest early on and that there was no distinct breach between the country style of the Southampton house and Winterthur.

By 1929 he had collected objects of such fine quality, especially furniture, that they are still considered masterpieces today. He was able to contribute one-sixth of the loans to the Girl Scout Loan Exhibition. Du Pont had assembled the core of the collection before the plans for Winterthur were finalized and the nature of these objects influenced other acquisition decisions. His collection grew also in response to the size, shape, and purpose of the rooms he was to furnish. Newly acquired furniture was photographed and general dimensions noted. In a process that paralleled the complicated designing of his gardens, he began to nurture the personality of particular spaces at Winterthur. Seating furniture was covered with plain muslins before joining tables, stands, and the case

*Detail of an embroidered panel from Philadelphia, 1754. Made by Mary King. Silk, metal thread, and glass beads, 18¼ x 24⅛"*

135

pieces in storage. When final room locations could be assigned, the appropriate historic fabrics could then be used without the waste of re-covering and losing precious inches of difficult-to-secure fabric. Anyone who has redecorated a single room, worrying about choosing readily available modern textiles and fringes and coordinating color schemes of carpets and curtains, can appreciate the complications of doing this without having the objects or their intended room locations available.

In August 1929, he engaged the firm of Ernest Lo Nano in New York City to do his upholstery and draperies. Noting that there would be "fully 100 side chairs to cover; 8 or 10 sofas; from 8 to 10 wing chairs and as many arms, and...about 40 pairs of curtains to be made, lined, etc. etc.," he made clear his expectations from the craftsmen he employed. "I shall want some of your best and most careful workmen, as these materials are all epoch pieces, extremely rare and valuable, and I could not afford to have any of them badly cut or put on or cut for the wrong chair." Because of delays in construction this work was not immediately undertaken. By the time the final layout of the house began there were numerous additional objects to be upholstered.

Despite the paucity of models, du Pont hoped not only to achieve a stylish ensemble but also to create accurate interiors. He still felt somewhat unequal to the task and had retained Sleeper to advise on fabrics, colors, and accessories, but the aging Boston decorator was unable to pay close attention to the project. Du Pont must also have realized Sleeper's inability to go beyond his own decorating taste. He wrote Sleeper in October 1930 and asked him to come down to Winterthur with photographs

*Sofa (top) from Salem, Massachusetts, 1800–10. Mahogany. Length: 71". Attributed to Samuel McIntire. Armchair (above right) from Boston, 1725–40. Oak and maple. Height: 43". Easy chair (above left) from Philadelphia, 1760–75. Mahogany, yellow pine, white oak. Height: 45". Embroidered panel (opposite) same as page 134. Full view*

and prints of old curtains so they might choose appropriate models and colors. He noted, "I am doing the house archeologically and correctly, and I am paying the greatest attention to the epoch of the fringes. I am very clear in my mind about the curtains and general line of coloring for several of the rooms, and, with that in view, started painting some two weeks ago after you were unable to come."

Light was important in the overall scheme. Although sconces and candle arms had a long tradition of use, the rise of gas and then electric lighting had made fixtures attached to the wall and chandeliers especially prominent in interior design. Du Pont went against tradition by having period lighting devices electrified in planning Chestertown House and Winterthur. He returned several dozen reflector lights to Charles Woolsey Lyon six months after their purchase, explaining: "I have been fiddling and fussing with my plans trying to place them advantageously with no success, and after seeing my sister's house here with no side lights whatsoever, I have decided to follow her example and to use lamps and an occasional chandelier as I think in that way you get more of an atmosphere of an old house."

Subtle shading and close alignment of hues were sought after in the house as well as in the gardens. He preferred the grayed and bleached tones of the old color surviving on period woodwork and evolved color washes to match them, rather than painting a room in strong modern pigments. Obtaining the right color effect was as much of a challenge as securing the right species for an area in the garden.

After du Pont returned from a visit to the great houses of Virginia

in late 1932, he wrote his guide: "Do you think it would be humanly possible to get a color of the paint in the living room at Shirley, showing the green baseboard? I would naturally pay for the man's time who would do it, and I should be glad as well to pay for the privilege of procuring that color."

A passage from a letter written at the end of the decade when du Pont was doing a new room in the house suggests the precision of his approach. Apologizing to a dealer for the delay in deciding on a certain fabric, he noted:

> In regard to a lot of silk and wool double cloth in rose and tan, are you sure that this lot is 18th century, and is it Italian or Spanish or what?
>
> The reason I am so slow about deciding is that my room has not yet been installed and I have to try out these pieces in another room with similar light, which means taking out the furniture in one end of the room, putting down the rug which is to go in the new room, and trying out the materials, so you see it is a difficult matter to decide. Furthermore, I am not sure if I am going to get another sofa for the room, which would mean a difference in the yardage of material I would require.

Accommodating modern facilities in period rooms proved similarly vexing. Light switches were to be buried in door jambs, telephones hidden in closets, preferably in positions so that they could not be seen when a door was opened. Radio speakers were hidden behind ceiling grilles that duplicated the effect of central plasterwork medallions. Even bathrooms were scrutinized to achieve the most harmonic relationship with adjacent period rooms. Du Pont wrote to Sleeper in 1929: "I am sorely troubled over the question of bathroom tiles. I have been living with some different colored tiles in my room for the past months trying to decide whether I should like them in my bathrooms or not." Sleeper responded:

> In regard to your bathroom tiles; I do not much like tiles in bathrooms that have any proximity to old rooms; not that they are much worse than the inevitable plumbing fixtures themselves, but I prefer and use where I can cork tile floors which look like old hard wood floors and have the advantage of being warm and I use with them just painted walls. As the latter have a simpler look they seem a little more consistent with old rooms. In some cases if I do not wish to paint the bathroom walls the color of the room walls, I make an attractive color combination of the bathroom based on the color of the curtains or on some predominating cheerful color in the curtains used in the rooms themselves. This would give the bathroom some logical relation to the rooms as to color, and perhaps make them a little more cheerful. I do not like white plumbing very much. As you know, now the fixtures come in a good many charming colors; several shades of green, cafe au lait, deep rose, and various blues, etc.

But besides this letter and a few occasional suggestions as to accessories, Sleeper's contributions to Winterthur were not significant. Du Pont finally terminated his contract with Sleeper in 1931 and remarked peevishly:

> You were unable to come the first time I wanted you, on October 29th [1930], and consequently as the time was very short I had to

*Glass taperstick (opposite) from Wistarburgh, Alloway, Salem County, New Jersey, 1739–77. Height: 4⅜." High chest (left) from Philadelphia, 1765–80. Cuban mahogany, tulip, white cedar, oak, yellow pine. Height: 90¼." Originally owned by John or William Turner and subsequently by the Van Pelt family. Basket (above) from Philadelphia, 1769–72, by Bonnin and Morris. Probably soft-paste porcelain. Diameter: 8"*

more or less decide upon the colors of three of my important rooms. When you did come and I spoke to you about having drawings made of period curtains, etc., you told me that your office was not equipped to do anything like that and that doubtless Lo Nano could find what I wished. As Lo Nano is an upholsterer he was not qualified to find period curtains suitable for my house. Therefore, I had to spend a great many hours of time in research, looking through the Metropolitan Museum, and public library books, in addition to having the illustrations photostated, etc. On one of your visits when I left you here I asked you to go over the few remaining curtains not decided upon with Lo Nano. All he had to show me after you left were four or five little pencil sketches which were so vague that, in fact, they were nothing...since your last visit here on the 21st of January the whole load of fixing the house has fallen upon me. In other words, the placing of the furniture, the hanging of pictures and mirrors, the arrangement of the rugs, and in fact every detail that was not furnished, fell upon me.

Although he complained to Sleeper, he must have genuinely enjoyed the task that was the fruition of years of careful planning and eager collecting. He had toured antique shops regularly, studied their contents, and stored them away in his vast memory. Often weeks or months later, recalling an object of a certain size, shape, or color that he thought he could now use, du Pont would inquire as to its availability. And as word of his collecting activities traveled, he was flooded with offers from owners and dealers across the country and from abroad. While he did not have agents scouring the countryside for antiques, as did Henry Ford, he did come to

rely on a steady supply from a variety of sources. Many of the important accessories came from J.A. Lloyd Hyde, who traveled abroad in search of glass, ceramics, and textiles that would appeal to du Pont. Export porcelains came from dealers in England and especially from Edward Crowninshield, his brother-in-law's cousin.

Du Pont's purchases were diverse. He actively bought from such local dealers as Francis Brinton, Lillian Berkstresser, Hattie Brunner, Joe Kindig, Jr. A directory of his purchases provides a lexicon of the most distinguished dealers in American antiques: Ginsburg and Levy, Israel Sack, Charles Woolsey Lyon, Nancy McClelland, George and Helen McKearin, Elinor Merrill, Ensko, and later Charlotte and Edgar Sittig, John Walton, Harry Arons, Charles Montgomery, and David Stockwell. He also scanned catalogues of collections, writing the owners in hopes of liberating an object; he perused auction catalogues, bidding at sales at the Anderson Galleries and the American Art Association. He poured over *The Magazine Antiques*, marking objects of interest or ones relating to pieces already in his collection on the magazine's cover and penned inquiries to dealers regarding their wares. As the telephone was rarely used for such purposes, the correspondence with dealers and specialists forms an invaluable guide to the developing antiques trade in America.

Even before du Pont began laying out the Winterthur rooms, he had the chance for a dry run when he assumed responsibility for assembling the display at the Girl Scouts Loan Exhibition in 1929. He was a major lender but more important his taste and energy were recognized when the exhibition's organizer, Louis Guerineau Myers, asked him to assist with

*Tambour desk or lady's writing table with tambour shutters. From Boston, 1794–1804. Labeled by John Seymour and Son, Cabinet Makers, Creek Square. Mahogany inlaid with light wood, white pine, white elm. Height: 41½." One of du Pont's prize purchases at the Phillip Flayderman sale*

the display. Du Pont arranged the furniture in the Anderson Galleries rooms in roomlike settings dedicated to different style periods. The plush grandeur of fabric-lined halls was not allowed to overshadow the simple elegance of the American objects. Photographs of the galleries reveal the subtle juxtaposition and coordination of forms, allowing each to speak without dominating the rest—du Pont's trademark. He got so involved in the right look of the display that at one point he threw off his hat and coat and simultaneously directed the workmen and fiddled with the exact positioning of pieces himself. His didactic interest is also apparent in the display and he commented privately that the glass display, organized by the authority George McKearin, "would be much more interesting if it were displayed chronologically."

His role in the Girl Scouts Loan Exhibition is a clear assertion of the prominent position he had assumed in the American antiques field by 1929. That prominence was underscored later that year when du Pont paid a staggering record price for a piece of American furniture, the important Van Pelt high chest from the esteemed Reifsnyder collection. There might have been an excited buzz in the rooms of the American Art Association gallery as the end of the week-long sale approached and the legendary high chest—described by the editor of *The Magazine Antiques* as one of "the most perfectly conceived and executed highboys made in pre-Revolutionary Philadelphia"—was put on the block. The sale had already scored numerous records due to the wide reputation of the Reifsnyder collection. A so-called "sample chair" brought $15,000, and a carved mahogany wing chair scored a dazzling $33,000, but the greatest competition was for the high chest. Du Pont, bidding under the pseudonym of H.F. Winthrop, battled William Randolph Hearst for lot 696 and at 5:15 PM on April 27, he made the final winning bid of $44,000—a record for American furniture that was unsurpassed for years.

Within a few months of the Reifsnyder sale Phillip Flayderman's equally famous collection went on the block. Reifsnyder's collection had boasted strength in Philadelphia furniture, while the Flayderman collection was especially strong in fine and well-documented New England work. Du Pont, perhaps wary of letting anyone know too much about his specific interests in the sale, asked several dealers, including his customary agents Collings & Collings and the redoubtable Israel Sack, to look at different lots for him, and he had individuals from Buffalo, Boston, and Washington bid for him. He was determined to avoid the competition that his obvious presence would engender. Though wise in the ways of the market he could not resist pressing toward his desired goals. Du Pont bought the record object of the sale, a labeled Seymour tambour door secretary for $30,000 and paid just $1,000 less for a tea table made by John Goddard for Jabez Bowen which, according to the editor of *The Magazine Antiques*, "everybody knew...would create a sensation, but few, if any, expected...it would create so intense a rivalry." He summarized the qualities that du Pont must surely have recognized: "the Goddard table is as remarkable a masterpiece [as the Reifsnyder high chest]. The composition of its finely flowing lines presented problems in construction really greater than those which had to be surmounted by the designer of the highboy.... The pure beauty of form which he achieved in this tea table no more de-

mands the enhancement of foliate carving than the Venus de' Medici needs a grass petticoat."

Highly secretive about his collecting activities even to the point of obscuring his purchases from his family, du Pont was naturally concerned about public scrutiny of his actions. While the heady extravagances of Henry Ford with his buying sweep through New England were legend and the monumental reconstruction activity at Williamsburg was exciting popular interest, du Pont was exceedingly private. No photographs of Winterthur appeared in the press for decades, although the house was thoroughly documented with colored stereopticon photographs taken in 1935 and again in 1938. While he was known to the trade, he did not generally make extensive purchases at one time and often returned things for which he decided he had no use. Rarely did he explain the rejection or return of an object. His explanations ranged from a curt, "I have no place for this object," or an improbable, "I cannot afford it." He once responded to a dealer's request for an explanation of why he rejected some silver beakers belonging to an impoverished Newport church, revealing his overriding collecting philosophy:

> I returned the beakers because, when I put them with some other silver I have, they unfortunately did not look well with it at all. That is exactly the reason why I had them sent on approval, as it was impossible to visualize from a photograph just how these beakers would look with the silver I have. As you know, I have made it a rule never to buy anything, no matter how beautiful, how valuable or how unusual, which does not go well with what I already have.

*Windsor settee (opposite) from Massachusetts or Connecticut, 1775–1800. Oak, hickory, ash, birch. Width: 98½." Needlework (top): The Fishing Lady. From Barnstable, Massachusetts, 1748. Made by Sarah Warren. Silk and wool on linen. 25⅜ x 52⅜." Iron pipe tongs (far left) from Massachusetts, dated Sept. 22, 1740. Made by Joseph Chapin. Length: 22." Chest of drawers (center) from Newport, Rhode Island, 1765–75. Attributed to John Townsend. Mahogany, ash, tulip. Height: 34¼." High chest (left) from Bedford, New Hampshire, c. 1780. Shop of John Dunlap I, probably by William Houston. Maple, white pine. Height: 83¼."*

*Covered tureen (top) from Staffordshire, England, 1745–75. Earthenware. Height: 7¾." Silver tankard (center left) from Boston, 1772. Made by Paul Revere. Height: 8¼." Engraved "The Gift of Mary Bartlett Widow of Ephm Bartlett to the third Church in Brookfield 1768." Recorded in Revere's daybook for January 1772. Covered tumbler (left) from Frederick, Maryland, 1788. Made by John Frederick Amelung, New Bremen Glass Manufactory. Nonlead glass. Height: 12¼." Engraved "Floriat Commercium Charles Ghequiere and New Bremen Glasmanufactory [sic] the 20th of June 1788." Figure of a lion (above) from Waynesboro, Pennsylvania, 1840–65. Made by John Bell. Lead-glazed earthenware. Height: 7⅜." Tea canister (opposite) from Wrightstown, Bucks County, Pennsylvania, 1796. Lead-glazed earthenware with slip and sgraffito decoration. Height: 8¼." Incised "L. Smith TEA"*

As the depression deepened he became concerned that the extravagant purchases he was still capable of making, despite a certain necessary belt tightening, might be adversely received. In 1931, he wrote to Edward Crowninshield:

> You must also bear in mind that during these times, when I am really buying under compulsion, I wanted to purchase at the best possible price and I could not have thought of putting as much money as $8,000.00 in a Lowestoft set no matter what it matched. I would appreciate it very much if you would not mention this sale to anybody, as during these hard times, I really think one might forego the purchase of Lowestoft sets.

The following year he rejected a table that had been brought to him at Winterthur and showed the tug-of-war that must have colored any of his purchase decisions—the right object and the right place. He wrote a friend:

> Benjamin Flayderman brought me a very fine ball and claw foot Goddard card table. The carving on the knees is quite as good as that on the two Goddard tables I have in the reception rooms. It has been here a week and he is taking it away again tomorrow, as at this time I really cannot think of paying what he wants for it—namely $7,000. I haven't any special place to put it, so the parting is not as painful as if I had just the spot for it. Still I hate to see it go, as it is one of the very few authenticated American card tables. The four corners are slightly raised to hold cups, and there has evidently been a green cover on the table at one time, as you can see the marks of the baise on the wood.

When the table appeared in an auction catalogue a few months later, he commented, "It is certainly a peach, but too expensive for me unfortunately."

Most of du Pont's purchasing decisions were intuitive. The sense of scale, proportion, colors, and workmanship that he developed over long years of looking became his guide. He was in every sense a connoisseur but it was not a scientific connoisseurship he practiced. Since the rise of interest in American antiques, more material came to light, museum exhibitions and permanent displays provided reference points for study, and a few in-depth publications as well as such journals as *The Magazine Antiques* and *The American Collector* added research to the current state of knowledge. But vast territories were still unexplored. Pioneering professionals, principally curators in Boston, New York, and Philadelphia, began to unravel the tangled web of misattributions and misrepresentations, but professional advice was still hard to come by. The dealers, who were perhaps the most knowledgeable through practical experience with the wide range of American objects, were also canny and not always thorough in their inspection of objects or in their presentation of them. In addition to the normal mistaken identity of Irish and English provincial objects for their American cousins, there was intentional faking.

Despite the vast quantities of American antiques still in private hands and available at relatively cheap prices, the faking of antiques had been a fact of life since the late nineteenth century. Objects were frequently ascribed to owners and makers who had no real connection with them. Simpler forms were repaired and embellished with ornaments and carvings and totally new forms were invented out of the parts of old ones. Commercial reproductions were artfully disguised and lent the patina of age by being planted in old houses, and new pieces made to fill out a set of chairs or duplicate a table or chest became confused with the genuine period piece. To step into this quagmire of ignorance and duplicity took fortitude and perseverance for the committed collector.

Du Pont was more than aware of this situation. As early as 1906, an article entitled "The Truth About Antique Furniture" had appeared in *Country Life in America*, to which he subscribed. In the chilling opening sentence, the author set a theme that was to be repeated over the years. "Probably not more than one piece in ten offered in the open market is at once genuine and in sufficiently good condition to be worth having." Although he was talking about English furniture, the same story would be told about American antiques.

Du Pont was wary and skeptical but he lacked the body of knowledge to fully dissect an object, relying more on instinct. He did, however, seek counsel from dealers, curators, and friends, and often bought a piece on condition of examination by an authority. He exercised that warranty and on occasion attempted to return an object as long as a decade after its purchase. During the late 1920's and early thirties, he frequently resorted to the dealers Collings & Collings for their expertise on furniture. In one case they reported back to his secretary after examining a chest at the storage warehouse:

> While at the Lincoln Storage Warehouse with him [Mr. du Pont] on Wednesday afternoon he had a crate opened up to show me a lowboy

*Looking glass from Philadelphia, 1770. Made by James Reynolds. White pine, yellow pine, tulip, paint, and gilt. Height: 55½." Made for John Cadwalader*

he had recently acquired. He said he knew the family it had come down in and there could be no question of its being original and I did not examine it as on its face it looked original and good, and I did not question it.

Today however I had occasion to take our man over to fit some keys to another piece of furniture and again I looked at the lowboy. Opening the top drawer my suspicions were aroused and we made a careful examination of the piece and found it to be practically a new piece of furniture. The fronts of the drawers are made of new wood and the linings from old drawer sides and bottoms. The legs and the sides of the piece are made of new wood. The top is made of old wood and has the old finish on it, and just the edges are finished new. The piece may have been made up five years or so ago but it could have been made yesterday.

On another occasion they wrote:

The table and the dressing case came in yesterday. The table both from the walnut and the gum wood used in its construction as also from the turnings in the legs looks to me to be French. Certainly it is not American. The dressing case is positively English.

Du Pont himself was a thoughtful observer and became increasingly confident of his own judgments. He returned a chair to a New York dealer in 1931 noting:

I have decided to return to you the New England Chippendale mahogany wing chair, because, in my opinion, the rails making up the base have been taken from an old bed and the holes where the ropes went through have been plugged up. The legs and stretchers also,

*High chest (left) from Massachusetts, probably Boston, 1725–40. Possibly by William Parkman. Walnut. Height: 86⅛." Chest-on-chest (right) from Newport, Rhode Island, 1765–80. Townsend-Goddard School. Mahogany, chestnut, white pine. Height: 96"*

apparently, are not original but were made from old wood, and the wings probably came from another old chair.

Chastened by this experience, the dealer offered another piece the following week, remarking:

> On approval we are sending you the Cherry lowboy, but we wish to call your attention to the fact that after examining this lowboy we find that it has a new top, reconstructed drawers and new handles. It seems that this lowboy has been repaired a long time ago.
>
> I am very sorry that I have not noticed that before I showed it to you, but from now on every piece will be thoroughly examined before we send it to you. We will also call your attention to every detail.

In 1930, Israel Sack wrote du Pont requesting his support for legislation that would make faking a criminal offense. Faking was not confined to furniture and indeed the difficulties of detecting frauds increased with ceramics and glass. As products of a reproductive technology, molded glass and ceramics were readily duplicated and handworked forms could be convincingly produced with only slightly more energy. In the country arts and Pennsylvania German production, for which du Pont had a long affinity, the continuity of craft traditions added to the pitfalls of connoisseurship. In such instances, the history of the object became its principal verification. Writing to one of his frequent suppliers of Pennsylvania German objects, Hattie Brunner, du Pont queried:

> The slip bottle has arrived safely and, before buying, I would like to know whether you got it from a private family. There is so much of this stuff floating around that it is very difficult to tell half the time if it is American or foreign. I don't think this looks strictly Pennsylvania, as a bottle I bought a year ago was so distinctly Pennsylvania that there was absolutely no question about it. In my opinion, a purchase of this kind depends so much on where it comes from, its history, etc.

For high-style wares, added decoration could fool even the most practiced eye. A widely publicized event of the period involved a rare set of Chinese export porcelain with the arms of New York State. The earlier decoration had been ground off the china, and the glaze had been polished, and new ornament was added. In the face of such perils, du Pont once remarked to Crowninshield: "It's so much pleasanter to hear about those fakes before purchasing than afterward."

Du Pont was a diligent student and despite his own aesthetic emphasis, was also concerned with authenticity. He became equally attentive to the regional and historical accuracy of the rooms he was creating. Although he was an independent and decisive person, he continued to rely on the counsel and advice of those he trusted. Through his correspondence and his travels, he developed an informal network of advisers. As his knowledge of antiques deepened, he became more selective in his choices as well as with those with whom he discussed them.

Curators from the Metropolitan Museum, including Charles O. Cornelius, C. Louise Avery, and later Joseph Downs, as well as specialists in other institutions, were corresponded with. He traveled widely to view exhibits, see historic architecture, and search out objects that might enrich the collections. Even the pioneering editor of *The Magazine Antiques*, Homer Eaton Keyes, aided du Pont's efforts, providing information on specific objects and calling du Pont's attention to pieces that might be bought.

His reserved nature and patrician upbringing kept the trade at a distance, yet he respected their interest and invited major New York dealers and the favored country dealers to visit Winterthur. He relied on their knowledge gained through practical experience but understood the self-interest that could color their statements. Eventually, he got caught up in the gossip and repartee of the marketplace and his enjoyment of a certain lusty humor found sympathetic response from these quarters. In 1929, Collings & Collings reported: "It may interest you to know that the day before yesterday Henry Ford was here with his secretary and bought a bill of goods from Mr. Lyon amounting to, according to what Mr. Lyon says, One Hundred and fifty-three thousand dollars."

He responded: "I am interested to hear about Mr. Ford's purchase. Mr. Lyon told me he had a very large sale, but he always makes such exaggerated statements that I paid no attention to him."

Du Pont fondly remembered his childhood wanderings around the barns and greenhouses of Winterthur and had a special affection for the estate workers and for the country art dealers who, while canny, were born of the same soil as the objects they sold and seemed to possess an integrity of place. The Quaker Francis D. Brinton was welcomed to Winterthur, and Hattie Brunner invited du Pont to a hearty Pennsylvania German repast in exchange for her welcome to Winterthur. Du Pont enjoyed her table and wrote afterward for the recipe for her noodles.

Among the legion of dealers who passed through his life, however, none played a larger role than Joe Kindig, Jr., from York, Pennsylvania. Within weeks of their first meeting they were on a first-name basis and du Pont wrote appreciatively:

> I was much interested in what you say about your house, and I should like to come and see it at the first opportunity. Would you mind telling me what your "vivid" colors are, and if it would fit in my scheme, would you allow me to copy the color for my house here? I think you are one of the few art dealers I know who are really interested in having an antique background, and I hope to have the pleasure of having you come to my Southampton house next summer as I know you will enjoy seeing it, also my house in Delaware when it is finished.

Kindig and du Pont formed a close friendship and had an easy dialogue concerning objects and their quality and authenticity. The naturally taciturn du Pont had open discussions with Kindig and the latter sought to guide and instruct and naturally offered du Pont the best of what his wide-ranging and resourceful scouting uncovered. The files at Winterthur are crammed with correspondence between the two. Kindig enthusiastically described the variety of objects—from handkerchiefs to guns—that he came across and du Pont eagerly looked forward to visits where new discoveries were unveiled.

The separation of family life and antiquing that clouded a certain amount of his activity was referred to in one letter to Kindig:

> I was also much interested to hear about your Martha Washington

sewing table. Will it be too late for you to wait until the week of July 17th to bring these pieces down, as it is hopeless for me to look at antiques when the family is here.

Kindig sold du Pont many of his finest pieces including nearly 20 percent of the pieces subsequently published in Joseph Downs's first Winterthur catalogue, *American Furniture: Queen Anne and Chippendale Periods*. Despite his closeness to du Pont he was a practical businessman and could take a hard line. When things were especially tight, he might suggest a swap, such as he did in May 1932 when he proposed trading some furniture for a cast-off Buick that du Pont, as an officer of General Motors, might have available. Du Pont had only just traded in his Buick but he replied: "I think the trade you suggest is what we are all going to do before long in one way or another, and it is not a dumb suggestion at all." He then added a postscript: "I have plenty of livestock of all kinds which I would gladly exchange."

Three months later Kindig produced a rare Philadelphia sofa with a history of ownership by the Delaware patriot John Dickinson, who authored *Letters from a Farmer in Pennsylvania* (Delaware was originally the Three Lower Counties of Pennsylvania). Kindig was asking $20,000— in the depths of the depression. Du Pont tried to bargain and Kindig flatly rejected any offer. He gave du Pont a deadline after which he would add the prized sofa to his own collection and suggested that if du Pont capitulated after the deadline he hoped he would understand if Kindig said no. "Your sofa is a perfect knockout and I shall never be happy until I own it," was du Pont's reply. A year later he finally weakened and sent the first

*Card table from Philadelphia, 1765–80. Mahogany, white cedar, white oak. Height: 27⅜"*

installment of a year-long payoff. While the family was away, the sofa was delivered without fanfare in the hopes that this extravagance might escape special attention.

An unusual levity seems also to have characterized the relationship between Kindig and du Pont and a tantalizing bit of buffoonery is hinted at in another note:

> Could you send me an extra print of that photograph you took of me in the telephone closet as my family think it is one of the best that have yet been produced? When you come down on the 16th (come in time for lunch if you like) I shall pose for you there again, without a hat and without glasses, as I feel that my beauty will be enhanced without these extra adornments!

Kindig realized the importance of du Pont's project and reveled in the range and quality of the collection. He wrote appreciatively and with a certain characteristic lament that du Pont's achievement had made collecting in the future more difficult since he had already secured so many gems. Du Pont responded with a compelling reflection on his own work and in one of the few intimate revelations in the thousands of surviving letters wrote:

> Many thanks for the receipted bills and for the nice things you say about my collection. I sincerely hope that it may never be dispersed; but if it has to be, I hope you will be at the sale and get some of the things you would like to have.
>
> I am sorry that it makes you feel depressed, as one of the joys of having the furniture in the right setting is to give pleasure to other people as well as to myself.

*Pier table (above) from New York, 1805–10. Made by Charles-Honoré Lannuier. Mahogany with satinwood and rosewood inlays, white pine, brass moldings. Height: 37." Labeled "Honore Lannuier, Cabinet Maker (from Paris) keeps his Ware-house and Manufactory and cabinet ware of Newest Fashion, at No. 60 Broad-Street." Side chair (opposite) from Philadelphia, 1685–1700. Black walnut. Height: 50⅜"*

I quite understand your mixed feelings, but don't you think it is partly just the fact that you have been away and had a good time and that when you come back to your own house you feel somewhat let down? I know very frequently—not so much now, but when I was young—when I went away and came back home I had exactly the same feeling. However, I enjoyed your visit very much. So in your life's account book just put down your trips as giving pleasure to H. F. du Pont.

Charles O. Cornelius was also closely associated with the completion of Winterthur's first expansion under du Pont. As a trained architect who had been closely associated with the American Wing at the Metropolitan and had served for a time as its curator, he was more intimately familiar with American historical architecture than Albert Ely Ives. Cornelius, like Sleeper, seems to have been unable to deliver work up to du Pont's standards. During 1932, when Cornelius was unemployed and looking for architectural jobs, du Pont hired him to prepare detailed room descriptions that would form the nucleus of the catalogue of the collection, a project that du Pont had originally planned with Cornelius for Chestertown House but which was now overshadowed by the importance of Winterthur. Du Pont described the project in some detail to Cornelius:

About this house: I want to turn out a very special book something along the lines of the one gotten up by the late Mr. J. P. Morgan, or possibly along the lines of McQuoid's "History of English Furniture." Perhaps the first part of the book would portray the beauty of the house and its more intimate surroundings, then the various

rooms as a whole, and then, insofar as possible in their order, the most beautiful, as well as rare, individual pieces, by chapters. The book, of course, would be fully illustrated, containing most if not all of my collection. The thing I want you to do principally will be the writing and writing up the whole thing.

Du Pont had misgivings about Cornelius from the beginning:

Dear Charles, don't think that I am trying to drive a hard and desperate bargain with you, but you have always been so delightfully vague in the past and I have had such poor results with the Southampton cataloguing that I am really a bit leery about all you charmingly artistic people.

There must certainly have been a bit of charity in the commission, and as with many of his activities during the depression du Pont hoped to cast a veil of secrecy over the catalogue, extending even to his own family. He enjoined Cornelius to remain silent and especially not to tell Mrs. du Pont about the work: "I know that Ruth will think this is a terrible piece of extravagance and I am scared to tell her about it, so please keep the whole matter dark until I say you can talk about it."

By December it was clear that Cornelius was not up to the work and du Pont wrote to his closest and most important confidant, Mrs. Harry Horton Benkard, for counseling in dealing with Cornelius on what was destined to be an aborted early attempt at cataloguing Winterthur:

Do you think I should write him a letter bawling him out for a very sloppy performance and also for doing this last room instead of

*Painted side chair (opposite) probably from Philadelphia, c. 1796. Maple and pine. Height: 38⅜." Pitcher (above) from Philadelphia, 1833. Made by Joseph Hemphill. Porcelain. Height: 8½." Signed on the bottom after Hemphill had taken full control of William Ellis Tucker's pioneering American porcelain manufactory*

155

doing my bedroom which is on the floor directly above? Or do you think that I should write him a sarcastic letter, or a pleasant letter, on the subject, or not mention it at all?

This letter shows the important role that Mrs. Benkard played in the planning and evolution of Winterthur. In fact, Bertha Benkard was so inextricably involved in the work at Winterthur that she might also be considered coauthor of the project.

Du Pont relied on Benkard for important judgments about objects. She was a distinguished collector in her own right, and acquired a fine grasp of late eighteenth- and early nineteenth-century furniture, much of it made by Duncan Phyfe and his circle in New York. Important pieces from her collection are in the Metropolitan Museum of Art, and in the Museum of the City of New York, where she directed the installation of a room in memory of her husband, the latter funded by Louise Crowninshield, who had been a lifelong friend of Bertha Benkard.

Du Pont frequently sent photos of pieces he had been offered for her consideration and expertise. Early in their correspondence it is clear that du Pont was the eager student and Benkard the knowledgeable authority. For instance, in 1929 he forwarded a photograph of a chair to her, inquiring, "I... should like to know if it is Phyfe and whether it is really a good type of Phyfe."

During the next decade his own knowledge would outstrip Benkard's but they were constantly in touch over the many details of selecting and placing objects, choosing proper colors, and appropriate architectural treatment. The endless search for fabrics and the task of overseeing upholstery- and curtain-making fell heavily on Benkard and she spent hours at Lo Nano's inspecting the work. After making an initial selection of textiles, du Pont would instruct her to "pick out any of the chintzes you like and tell Lo Nano to make up the curtains" or ask her, "If in your wanderings you should see 20 yards of pale green material, do seize it for me, as I know it will be perfectly all right."

She traveled to Winterthur during his frequent long absences to take charge of the work or review his decisions. She would find detailed multipage lists of assignments that reveal the complexity of the simultaneous completion of so many rooms. He asked her to examine the location of objects and regroup furniture, move pictures, mirrors, and sconces or make adjustments in the position of china and other decorations. He suggested that in one room she "paint any color that will go well with the blue of the curtain," and later he requested "before the West Room is definitely finished, could you manage to come down with Mr. Campbell and look at it and if the color is not just right, change it to anything you think will be right." These notes suggest a casual attitude toward the finished effect, but they should be understood as a reflection of the complete faith he had in Benkard's judgment as properly mirroring his own ideas.

He often quoted her judgments to dealers, decorators, craftsmen, and architects and used her opinion as the ultimate fine screen of approval. When the plans for a later renovation were delayed, he pressed the architect: "Please be sure that the other blueprints, of the hall, etc. are here by Saturday night, as Mrs. Benkard is coming only for the day on Monday and I shall be frantic if they are not here for her to see." Together

*Coverlet from Philadelphia, 1780–1800. Attrib-
uted to John Hewson. Block-printed cotton. 106¼
x 106¼"*

they poured over and over the detailed arrangements and seemed never to have seriously disagreed on any points.

In discussing the plans for redoing a room in the older part of the house, he also revealed their shared sense of propriety:

> In regard to using door No. 7 for the Nemours Room, it strikes Mrs. Benkard and me that the little rosette is applied plaster and nothing else in the Nemours Room suggests plaster. It seems to me that it belongs to a more sophisticated period than the woodwork in the Nemours Room.

And subsequently he informed the architect:

> I have ordered the entablature for the Nemours Room and Mrs. Benkard will decide when the room is finished whether to put it on or leave it off. The only reason I might want to leave it off is that I do not want to gild the architectural lily.

Du Pont willingly acknowledged Benkard's contribution to Winterthur when he remarked: "Without the expert advice and absolutely faultless taste and eye of Mrs. H. H. Benkard, who has given hours of her time unstintingly, the results never could have been accomplished."

Although du Pont was well known as a collector and the enormity of his project could have been surmised from the gossip of dealers who were only too eager to recount their latest sale, very little was known about Winterthur except by du Pont's closest friends and intimates. The long construction period of the wing and the complicated details of final room arrangements as well as the sudden availability of many fine objects brought out by economic pressures all delayed the point at which du Pont finally considered the house finished. By mid-July 1931, however, du Pont, writing the distinguished collector and frequent competitor Francis P. Garvan, suggested that he had about finished with collecting: "In the way of furniture, all I need is two small early pine tables with two legs and a stretcher between, a small size Chippendale bed, and a very small ball and claw foot table." He quickly amended this rather bald statement, adding, "Of course I might fall for some unusual piece of furniture that might turn up."

Considering the volume of subsequent purchases, this was a classic understatement but at the moment du Pont was content. He had built his American wing, furnished it with premier examples of the seventeenth-, eighteenth-, and early nineteenth-century craft of America, and placed it in an unrivaled architectural and natural setting. He concluded his letter to Garvan with an invitation to visit in the autumn.

Du Pont was not only at home at Winterthur, he was at home with his peers in the collecting field, the principal among them being Garvan. Garvan had in fact written du Pont with an interesting proposition. Reflecting on the state of the market and the collapse of competitive interest engendered by the depression and the flood of fine objects that had been the result of economic pressure, he inquired, "Can we not come to some understanding?" Garvan had been collecting since the mid-1910's and had assembled some ten thousand objects that while of high aesthetic standard were intended to form the nucleus of a teaching collection. He sought to create a well-rounded body of objects that would be "available to the en-

tire country and open up instruction and research on them." By the time he wrote to du Pont in June 1931, his collection had been the property of Yale University for a year. Garvan was attempting to fill in the outlines of the American artistic chronicle and particularly to enhance the finest single collection of American silver. He confided to du Pont:

*Bed rug from Colchester, Connecticut, 1778. Made by Mary Foot. Wool. 103½ x 77½"*

Apparently we are the only two purchasers of American antiques left in America, and I am a purchaser only to the most limited extent, and I feel that we are being used to our mutual disinterest. I am not interested in anything except prints and silver, and very little in prints. Practically, I am only interested in completing the educational exhibit of silver at Yale. It is most comprehensive and I would like to complete that one job so that that art be secured for historical preservation and study. However, whenever I want a piece I am threatened with it being sold to Mr. du Pont if I do not pay an extravagant price for it, and undoubtedly the same thing is being said to you.

Du Pont responded that he would of course like to avoid such competition and "After seeing your superb collection at New Haven, I naturally do not

wish to stand in your way to make it as complete as possible."

Du Pont had in fact turned down a silver paten that had prompted Garvan's letter. He needed only a few tankards "that might look well on a gateleg table" and had only acquired silver "for decorative purposes." As for the other antiques in addition to the furniture mentioned above, du Pont only lacked "two 18th century prints or engravings that are wider than they are high."

In his reply, Garvan asked for specific dimensions for the pictures but, more importantly, instructed du Pont:

> If I were you I would buy the paten at $4,000.00. This is $2,000.00 cheaper than it would have cost me, after I paid commissions, because I was offered it at $5,000.00 and commissions. For your purpose, to use on the table, I consider one paten worth three tankards. They are of course infinitely rarer than tankards. We have seventy-two tankards in the New Haven collection and only two or three patens. I admit I only paid $1,200.00 for mine years ago, but if I did not have it I would pay the $4,000.00 gladly. With me definitely out—and I have announced to them I am definitely out—you may be able to bargain for less, but it is such a well-known piece and so useful as a center piece for your table, I would not hesitate. If times were good I would buy it for my own use at home, but I cannot afford anything except the completion of the New Haven historical collection.

The dialogue between Garvan and du Pont is a perfect expression of the differences between a domestic and a didactic approach to collecting. Even though du Pont had a plan for the museumization of Chestertown House, the idea of opening Winterthur to the public was probably still taking shape in his subconscious. After an exhausting and costly three-year campaign he should have been quite content to enjoy his creation. But pressures were building. He had assumed center stage in the collecting field.

*Benjamin West. American Commissioners of the Preliminary Peace Negotiations with Great Britain, c. 1783. Oil on canvas, 28⅜ x 36⅛." This unfinished painting includes portraits of (left to right) John Jay, John Quincy Adams, Benjamin Franklin, Henry Laurens, and William Temple Franklin*

The Montmorenci staircase was removed from a
c. 1822 house in Shocco Springs, North Carolina,
where it was a single, circular flight. In adapting it
to Winterthur, du Pont and his architect, Thomas
T. Waterman, using period precedents, altered
the design to an elliptical plan and added a second flight. The Montmorenci staircase is a perfect
expression of the spidery geometry of the neoclassicism that replaced the bold forms of the colonial
period. Even the Palladian window of the upper
landing shows a linear and attenuated grace, contrasting with the massive detailing of the Palladian windows from Port Royal on the front and
garden doors of the 1928–31 wing. The rooms in
this color section were installed in the 1902 wing,
which during the 30's was remodeled to house
period interiors

161

The Marlboro Room (above and right) was so large that it required woodwork from two eighteenth-century rooms in Patuxent Manor, a house built in Lower Marlboro, Maryland. Its more than forty-five pieces of furniture are organized into discrete groupings and feature a number of unique forms or pieces that were newly introduced in their style period. In the room are such rare forms as a Queen Anne sofa and a matched set of Philadelphia stools, and such specialized forms as the two New York roundabout chairs commonly used with a desk. Two paintings by Charles Willson Peale include a portrait of Richard Bennett Lloyd and a rare group portrait of the Edward Lloyd family with a view of their Maryland plantation, Wye House

In contrast to the adaptation of historic woodwork in the Marlboro Room, the Flock Room (above and left) is one of the most accurately installed period interiors. Du Pont had owned the painted overmantel for many years before he succeeded in acquiring the remaining woodwork from Morattico Hall, c. 1715, in Virginia, and the flocked canvas wallcoverings made to emulate costlier velvets used as wallcoverings in Europe. The furniture demonstrates the importance of the cabinetmaker, who replaced the carver, joiner, and turner of the seventeenth century. The William and Mary style is commanding and sculptural, as is readily identified by the spiral turnings of the table legs, andirons, and other pieces in the room. Finer, richly figured veneered woods replaced the coarser carved oak of the Pilgrim era, suggesting a new sense of worldliness

163

The transition of furniture making from a small, custom-order business to an industry is evident in the Phyfe Room (above, right, and opposite). In addition to producing furniture on order, Duncan Phyfe kept a warehouse of ready-made cabinetwork, including ten side chairs and two armchairs sold to William Bayard. Phyfe may well have provided the case for the piano. Decorative bands were incorporated into handsome silver tea and coffee sets, such as the Philadelphia Chaudron and Rasch example shown here. Phyfe, who was born in Scotland, was one of the legion of émigré craftsmen who found opportunity in America as was the French-born Eleuthère Irénée du Pont, whose daughters Victorine and Eleuthera were painted by Rembrandt Peale

During the seventeenth and eighteenth centuries, design influences in America came principally from England. The black transfer-printed tea set on the Philadelphia scalloped-top table in the Patuxent Room (left) was made in Worcester, England, and the design of the bracket on the far wall was copied directly from Thomas Johnson's influential publication of 1758. In the eighteenth century, bedrooms were frequently used for informal entertaining. Here a visitor would view high chests, easy chairs, and rich fabrics, such as these finely worked crewel-embroidered hangings with

pastoral landscapes. By the nineteenth century, France was competing with England as a major design influence, although French styles may have come in part through English interpretations. Such émigré craftsmen as Charles Honoré Lannuier, to whom the bed in the Nemours Room (top) is attributed, brought a French neoclassicism inspired by Napoleon's endorsement of the antique style. Formal parlors and other specialized spaces such as the Empire Parlor and Hall (above left and right) show the new elaborations of American life in the nineteenth century

Henry Francis du Pont orchestrated the interior of Winterthur as expressions of color and form. His interest in gardening, as suggested in the portrait by Aaron Shickler in Memorial Library (right), influenced his approach to the rooms in Winterthur. His coloristic approach is evident in the Queen Anne Dining Room (above), where the soft green woodwork from a mid-eighteenth-century house in East Derry, New Hampshire, forms the perfect background for an extravagant array of boldly shaped furniture and dramatic patterns of resist-dyed upholstery. Rare purple manganese-glazed delftware tiles, platters, and bowls add intensity to the color scheme. A large delft bowl with an inscribed tribute to the merchants of Boston, England, provides the hub for the circular shapes that dominate the design of the Queen Anne style in the room

The direct trade between France and America after the revolution was evident not only in the adoption of French-influenced neoclassical styles but also in the flood of imported goods. French block-printed scenic wallpapers represented the ultimate in skilled wallpaper manufacture and found their way into hinterland settlements in America as well as into the homes of the urban elite. A section of the Bay of Naples set made by Dufour, c. 1833, featuring cargo handlers makes an appropriate reference to the vital influence of international trade for the new nation. Included in the silver on the Baltimore-painted marble-topped pier table is a ewer by Samuel Kirk, whose Baltimore shop was a leader in repoussé design and manufacture of the period

169

Philadelphia had become the commercial center
of America by the mid-eighteenth century, and
her craftsmen were among the most skilled in the
colonies. The carving on Philadelphia furniture
is a benchmark of excellence, and the conforming
elegance of interiors is evidenced by the sophisticated detailing of the Blackwell Parlor (above
and right). Built in 1764 on Pine Street, the
house was constructed two years after Edward
Stiles' country seat, Port Royal, was completed.
This room provides an interesting contrast with
the adjacent Port Royal Parlor. Architectural
details in both are derived from English design-
book sources, but the carving in the Blackwell
Parlor is carried to a degree of elaboration that
suggests it was executed by carvers who were also
responsible for the best furniture work in the city.
The architectural carvings can be measured
against the finely carved Philadelphia pieces
shown here, especially the several examples of the
rare hairy paw foot. To the left of the doorway
leading to the Port Royal Parlor, John Singleton
Copley's austere rendering of Mrs. Roger Morris
provides a chastening accent. The Blackwell Parlor was installed in a service area, and during the
1930's other entertainment rooms and service
areas also gave way to specialized displays. The
Dancing Room and Ping-pong Room were
reworked into the Bertrand Room and the Tappahannock Room (opposite top left and right) and
Hall and were furnished with Pennsylvania and
New York William and Mary furniture. The Bert-

rand Room, with woodwork from Belle Isle, now
displays New York Chippendale furniture. The
bowling alleys, badminton court, and attic rooms
shelter specialized displays of Chinese export
porcelain, spatterware, and historical blue Staffordshire (opposite center left and right, bottom
left). A group of facades (opposite bottom right)
from Delaware, Rhode Island, North Carolina,
and Massachusetts form the courtyard with its
extensive collection of Windsor chairs and settees
and tavern furniture

The Winterthur collection has a concentration of high-style craft products and imported objects for the upper economic strata. But Henry Francis du Pont's earliest collecting enthusiasm was for country and regional arts, and he never lost his fascination with rural and simple city furnishings. The Pennsylvania German Bedroom (top) reflects a different aesthetic with its collections of brightly painted furniture and textiles. The painted bed is covered with an intensely colored spread in blue, orange, greens, and russets. Most such coverlets were the products of professional weavers rather than of home looms, as once believed. Everywhere evidences of daily life stand in counterpoint to the formal lessons of style influence and change. The Child's Room (above left) features a fully dressed child-size bed and a toy or miniature example at its foot with its original coverings, providing invaluable evidence of period practice. The Miniature Stair Hall (above right) contains hundreds of period miniatures of all aspects of a household, including such items as warming pans, cradles, fire buckets, dishes, baskets, and carpets

The furnishings of the pioneering settlers were rural products reflecting the cultural and economic background of those early immigrants. Such objects represent the continuity of folk and craft traditions brought from the Old World. A tradition of consumption and display accompanied the early settlers, who retained a preference for highly decorated objects in their new homes. Although many early pieces were stripped of the bright paint and decorations they once sported, examples at Winterthur still show the rich palette of pioneer life. The kas, or wardrobe, in the Hardenbergh Bedroom (upper left) reflects the baroque tradition of marquetry inlay reproduced here in paint. The portrait of Adam Winne, dated 1732, characterizes the limner tradition that flourished during the first half of the eighteenth century among the Dutch patroons in the Hudson River Valley. The court cupboard in the Hart Room (lower left) was the most elaborate form produced in seventeenth-century New England. Its turned and applied ornament, with decoration painted black to simulate ebony, conforms with its purpose as a vehicle to display ceramics and silver as trappings of status and wealth. This room from the Thomas Hart house, c. 1670, in Ipswich, Massachusetts, is furnished with a variety of forms, including a chest of drawers and a blanket chest attributed to Thomas Dennis or William Searle and suggests the multiple functions such rooms served during the earliest decades of settlement. The Oyster Bay Room (lower right), with woodwork from the Job Wright house of c. 1667 in Oyster Bay, Long Island, includes seventeenth-century furniture from New England and New York that was fashioned in the English tradition. The Dutch-derived kas contrasts with the flat-carved decoration of the adjacent blanket chest and Bible box. Exposed beams and plaster walls were often painted with either solid colors or bright patterned decoration. The continuing preference for painted woodwork in rural areas is seen in the Dunlap Room (upper right) from the Thomas Chandler house in Bedford, New Hampshire. A decorated corner cupboard from the house is filled with English pottery called Whieldon ware

Only a year after the Treaty of Paris ended the Revolutionary War, Americans ventured to join the lucrative China trade. Fine-bodied and durable porcelains from Canton were imported in huge sets with decorations that mirrored changing western styles. Emblazoned with the American eagle, the Ridgway set (above) contains 416 pieces and gives evidence that Winterthur has the largest collection of Chinese export porcelain made for the American market as well as significant groups made for various European markets

For centuries bedhangings provided privacy in common sleeping rooms and offered warmth and protection against drafts. By the late eighteenth century, improvements in heating and the multiplication of bedrooms reduced hangings to more decorative functions. The netted tester in the Winterthur Bedroom (above) and the sheer fabric in the Sheraton Bedroom (left) mirror the neoclassical taste for loose swags reflecting the filmy costumes of antiquity. The hanging in the Empire Bedroom (far left) was taken directly from a French magazine and shows the influence of such periodicals in the rapid advances of fashion. During the eighteenth century, the man played a leading role in decorating and design decisions, and the Architect's Room (overleaf) shows the gentleman's interest in architecture, mathematics, and natural philosophy

175

# FROM HOUSE
# TO MUSEUM

**D**u Pont occupied a peculiar position in the collecting world. He was able to combine extensive financial resources with an indefatigable energy and enthusiasm and a highly sophisticated aesthetic judgment. Although he was on the board of the Du Pont Company and also a board member of General Motors, he did not hold an active position in either company. While Ford and Rockefeller also had enormous wealth to dedicate to their collecting activities, they were more specifically the financiers of their collections and less involved in the details of acquisitions. At Williamsburg a large professional staff was in place and in Dearborn Ford was assembling volumes of objects ranging from craft productions to machinery and machine products and did not focus exclusively on decorative arts. The emphasis at Williamsburg and Dearborn was on history and interpretation of the chronicle of American civilization. Garvan furthered his educational purposes when he extended his collections for public display. He, too, was interested in the role of the craftsman in American history. From that interest he developed a strong aesthetic sense and a high level of discrimination in his collecting.

In addition to the fine art collections in museums, probably the strongest aesthetic approach to American decorative arts was to be found among the leading women collectors of the period—Mrs. J. Insley Blair, Mrs. J. Amory Haskell, and Bertha Benkard, to name a few. Their collections were select concentrations and did not encompass the quantities of the Rockefeller-Ford-Garvan-du Pont axis. Only du Pont had the particular combination of time and resources to assemble a premier collection. That he had done so was recognized by the select fraternity of American

collectors when he was elected in 1932 to the Walpole Society. That decision was the final confirmation of the eminent status he had reached as a collector.

The Walpoleans were worldly and convivial and du Pont's admission to their ranks not only secured his position in the collecting world but also gave him access to the group that possessed the same committed interest to the decorative arts on a national level. The qualifications for membership in the Walpole Society set out the clublike standards of the organization: "distinction in the collecting of early American objects of the decorative arts and the fine arts, or attainment through study or experience in the knowledge of these arts; and the social qualifications essential to the well-being of a group of like-minded persons."

Prominent among the membership were curators, antiquarians, and collectors, principally from New England. Given the more tangential interest in American decorative arts of Rockefeller and Ford, it is not surprising that neither one was nominated for membership. Garvan's absence from the roster is more surprising. The requirement of "social qualifications essential to the well-being of a group of like-minded persons" must surely have conspired to keep out the Irish-Catholic Garvan.

Conviviality was an important aspect of Walpolean activities, for the group organized far-flung visits to historic sites and collections, expanding their knowledge in a way that the still-limited museum displays

could not. They shared information, read papers, and published studies in addition to the occasional papers that appeared in their annual notebook. Although du Pont's attendance at meetings and tours was intermittent in the early years, he came increasingly closer to the Walpole circle. With the restrictions on travel imposed by World War II he became an active participant and was one of the few members who brought recent acquisitions along for general scrutiny. From the beginning of his membership, du Pont's achievement was recognized by the group. The reaction of his fellow Walpoleans when they first saw Winterthur in the fall of 1932 was enthusiastic and profuse.

> Imagine a house which records the decorative history of our Country, and that in supreme terms! Are you interested in architecture? Here you will see choicely chosen examples of interior woodwork covering two centuries. Is it silver? The finest examples of distinguished Colonial makers. Pottery? Everything the Country affords. Pewter and brass? A fine collection. Porcelain, especially that brought from the Orient by the East India Company? A bewildering array. Looking glasses? Fine specimens of every kind. Textile and needlework that show once more what beauty and color picked out the households of the Colonists.

The Walpoleans were well traveled and familiar with most of the important collections that had been put together in the twenty-three years since the society was founded. Their enthusiasm for Winterthur, therefore, was high praise indeed. They were overwhelmed by the quality, range, and diversity of the collection. They were equally impressed with the ensemble and the subtle ways in which du Pont had organized the objects into a harmonious and lively display.

It would be quite impossible to do justice to this collection in so

*Opposite: John Singleton Copley. Self-Portrait, 1769. Pastel on paper, 23⅛ x 17½." Members of the Walpole Society (above) in the garden at Winterthur on their first visit, October 14–16, 1932. Left to right: Pratt, Spalding, du Pont, Brainard, Fielding, Nash, Lockwood, Halsey, Isham, Richards, Dow, Weddell, Miller, and Goodwin*

St. Mémin fecit

short an account. As the visitors went from room to room, each one
with a background perfect for its period and locality, they saw superb examples of Queen Anne, Early and Late Georgian, all the
work of our own fine cabinet makers, Hartford, Boston, Newport,
Philadelphia, Baltimore and New York, and many other sections of
our country, where distinction in design or decoration gives us
knowledge of their geographic origin. Each room arranged with
endless care shows not only the main features of a period but the
detail of textile, needlework, floor covering, ornament and pictures.
The lighting has been carefully considered and the simulation of
candle light with small electric bulbs often on genuine candles has
been most successful.

Their special tribute was also a criticism of the museum curatorial approach that, while emphasizing American life as a background for American objects, lost the spark of that life in the frozen museum galleries. By
contrast at Winterthur "There is nothing of the museum in the air. We are
not among the dead."

Three weeks after the Walpole visit and possibly fired by the discussions during that meeting, du Pont decided to plan a tour of great
southern mansions. Du Pont wrote to Thomas Tileston Waterman, a young
draftsman employed on the Williamsburg project in the firm of restoration architects Perry, Shaw and Hepburn. Waterman was characteristic of
a new breed of scholarly and able young professionals who emerged in the
1930's and whose counsel du Pont sought. In November 1932 Waterman
was the ideal person to organize a tour for du Pont and Bertha Benkard.
In response to du Pont's assertion that he was a "pretty quick traveler,"

*Opposite: Charles B. J. Fevret de Saint-Mémin.*
*Osage Warrior, c. 1804. Watercolor on paper, 7½ x 6¾".*
*Bedspread (above) from India, 1690–1720.*
*Painted and resist-dyed cotton and linen, 106¾ x*
*148½"*

Waterman proposed an exhausting four-day expedition:

> The trip that I suggest is as follows. The first day York Hall, Old
> Point, Thoroughgood House, the Meyers House (Norfolk), St. Luke's
> Church, Bacon's Castle, Four Mile Tree, Brandon, Battersea and the
> night in Petersburg. The second day Shirley, Westover, Chelsea,
> Sweet Hall, Elsing Green, Wilton and Richmond for the night. The
> third day Blandfield, Brookes Bank, Elmwood, Gaymont, Kenmore
> (Fredericksburg), Chatham, Stratford, Menokin, Mt. Airy and Sa-
> bine Hall, the night at Richmond or Fredericksburg. The fourth
> day Rosegill, Toddsbury, Rosewell, Fairview, Carter's Grove,
> Greenspring and Williamsburg. This may prove more complete
> than you contemplated, and could, of course, be shortened.

Waterman may have expressed some anxiety about the purpose of the trip.
As an architectural historian he may well have been concerned over the
pillaging of historic buildings for paneling and architectural details. Perhaps in anticipation of Waterman's censure du Pont had assured him:

> My house here is entirely finished and my idea is not to look for pan-
> elling which I can buy. I simply want to see these lovely old houses,
> as I am particularly interested in the architecture of that time.

Waterman was almost immediately pressured into service to assist
with furniture acquisitions and would, within a few years, become the
principal architect for the 1930's remodeling of the 1902 wing at Winterthur. Du Pont must have felt the conflict between the new wing and the old
house almost immediately, and despite his protestations to the contrary
had probably formulated plans for redoing the old house. This incessant
collecting certainly created pressures on the available space in the wing
and his new discoveries and increasing enlightenment about previously
neglected areas of American decorative art all led inevitably to the con-
clusion that the old interiors must go.

An equally useful and important professional in the curatorial field
had emerged with du Pont's acquaintance with Joseph Downs. As Waterman had been the guide to the mansions of Virginia, Downs was to do the
same service in an extended motor tour of the Hudson Valley that du Pont
and Benkard made in the summer of 1933. On his return from Albany,
du Pont wrote to Waterman, then traveling on a European study tour:

> Joe Downs is going to have an exhibition of New York Chippendale
> furniture at the Metropolitan this winter and has been trying to
> borrow pieces right and left, so we saw no end of those pieces and I
> am beginning to know something about it now. It really is not any-
> where near as handsome as Philadelphia Chippendale, but the best
> types are very interesting. Then we saw lots of Phyfe furniture and
> some superb portraits in their original frames, good silver, and any
> amount of interesting architecture....

Downs, like Waterman, was characteristic of a new generation of
professionals who were succeeding the amateur enthusiasts as the custodians of the American artistic heritage. He was appointed the first curator of decorative arts at the Philadelphia Museum of Art in 1928 and
in 1932 he moved to the American Wing of the Metropolitan Museum.
Downs was a collector himself and a member of the Walpole Society. In
addition, he shared with du Pont a special interest in Pennsylvania Ger-

man arts. Downs was responsible, in fact, for the first formal installation of Pennsylvania German objects in both Philadelphia and New York and, ultimately, upon his appointment in 1949 as first curator of Winterthur, would supervise the first major display of similar material there.

Du Pont had been actively collecting Pennsylvania German material, including furniture and carvings, pottery and porcelain, and textiles and ironwork since the 1920's, and his proximity to the region made this material easily accessible. He frequently set off on automobile tours of the region with his driver and was always prepared to knock on the door of a likely farmhouse to inquire about a piece of furniture he might have spied on a porch or seen through a window. This catholicity as a collector is given no better evidence than in the range and quality of the Pennsylvania German collection. This was already evident when the Walpole Society made its first visit in 1932. Their description also suggests how unusual such material appeared even in these early days when American folk art and the vernacular tradition were just being understood.

> The Pennsylvania German room was of surpassing interest, especially to us New Englanders who have little acquaintance with the type. In a large fireplace there was a huge cast-iron fire-back with an inscription. These Germans brought their own crafts with them, and the flavor of them is distinctly different from those the English settlers brought, differences easily perceived but hard to describe.

The thirties were a great period in the development of the study of American folkways. American folk art had been recognized since the early twenties largely through the pioneering efforts of contemporary art-

*Shonk from Pennsylvania, probably Lancaster County. Dated "Feby 17, 1768." Black walnut and sulfur inlay. Height: 89½"*

ists who recognized a common thread of abstraction in these localized products. The aesthetic interest was broadened into a cultural one by the 1930's as folklorists continued to document and record stories and songs that had survived in American rural populations. Allan Lomax's work for the Library of Congress was supplemented by other documentary projects in art and architecture. The WPA writers project produced guides for each state, and the *Index of American Design* under Holger Cahill recorded in detailed watercolor renderings highlights of American rural and urban craft production. Du Pont understood the sophistication of country arts and when a cousin rejected a high-backed settee that Kindig had offered commented, "He thinks it is much too crude, and evidently has not been educated up to this type of furniture as yet." A display area with Pennsylvania German objects and one with the currently fashionable Stiegel glass were among those du Pont planned during the thirties as he prepared for "the great shift" in the 1902 wing.

Unlike the wing he had added to Winterthur, remodeling of the 1902 wing proceeded piecemeal as funds could be freed up and as appropriate architectural details became available. He was busy as early as 1933 installing woodwork from Patuxent Manor, a 1740's house from Lower Marlboro, Maryland, in the great Red Room west of the marble stair. He removed the fake beams and other components of the sham Renaissance style installed three decades earlier. As with the Chinese Parlor to the south of the stair hall, the Red Room was to be a major entertaining space and would serve as a background for furniture rather than reproduce a specific period room type. Du Pont concentrated objects of family history

*The Pennsylvania Folk Art Room (left) has collections of Pennsylvania German furniture, pewter, and sgraffito ware*

*Tall clock (left) from Elizabethville, Dauphin County, Pennsylvania. Dated 1815. Made by Johannes Paul, Jr. Curly maple and tulip. Height: 98″. Commons Room (above) with woodwork from Red Lion Inn, Red Lion, Delaware, early nineteenth century. This room includes a variety of Windsor chair forms from New England and Pennsylvania. The walnut dresser holds a collection of southern pewter*

and association in this room, which also served as a gathering place and a conversation area. On the floor immediately above the Red Room he employed woodwork from Patuxent in creating a more authentic period room of extraordinary elegance and sophistication. It was for this room that he had begged the privilege of acquiring a color from Shirley in his letter to Waterman in December of 1932. Other bedrooms were reworked with period architectural details and the small bathrooms at the northern terminus of the long central hall were eliminated to increase natural light at the dark intersection of the halls and to provide additional gallery space. Some rooms were modified by the elimination of closets and service areas. These and many other small adjustments were made to accommodate new woodwork and to create a more authentic effect. Most of the recreational rooms were eliminated to provide space for collections. The Billiard Room and Squash Court with their low ceilings (two floors were made of the Squash Court) and narrow proportions provided ideal spaces for rooms of the late seventeenth and early eighteenth centuries.

With each new area the changing over of the house to a museum became more apparent and the zeal with which du Pont pursued the projects makes clear what no written evidence documents—the intention to create a comprehensive museum collection at Winterthur. Du Pont's increasing concern with authenticity and historical accuracy is a testament to this purpose as well as to his own maturity in the field. His dependence on the best professional advice further defines the seriousness of his intention. Although he continued to look to Bertha Benkard for aid in the fine tuning of room arrangements and in the selection of accessories, he turned to scholars and professionals for help in locating precedents and prototypes for his architectural arrangements. The increase in scholarship of antiques also made greater accuracy in the choice of objects possible.

Du Pont's correspondence from the 1930's shows him wrestling with the often conflicting demands of aesthetics and authenticity. The dialogue often centers on details that might have easily been overlooked. One characteristic episode involves the reworking of the Chinese Parlor and the small room immediately to the south of it in which Chinese export porcelain from the Society of the Cincinnati (an exclusive group of retired Revolutionary War officers and their descendants) set was displayed. The Chinese Parlor was not really a period room but a setting carved out of several of the small rooms of the original Winterthur house. Its size was determined by the wallpaper it was to hold and its contents were arranged to show the variety of exotic influences on Chippendale furniture designs. As first installed, the room had an English mantelpiece and window and door surrounds designed for the ensemble. In June 1937, du Pont wrote to Albert Ely Ives, the original architect of the room and of the 1928–31 wing: "I have at last found an American Chippendale mantelpiece for the Wallpaper room [Chinese Parlor] which, though not so pretty as the English one, will be more appropriate." The installation of the mantel precipitated the redesign of the doorways and window surrounds. Du Pont resented the necessity of using modern woodwork. In 1934, he had commented on the plans for a house being designed for a cousin: "Inasmuch as he is using all new mantelpieces, new woodwork and new hardware, I cannot imagine that it will be anything very interesting."

Plate from Pennsylvania, possibly Montgomery
County, dated 1819. Initialed R.G., possibly
Rudolph Graber. Lead-glazed, drape-molded
earthenware with slip and sgraffito decoration.
Diameter: 12″. Seen against the painted wood-
work from the David Hottenstein house, 1783,
Kutztown, Berks County, Pennsylvania, installed
in the Fraktur Room

Du Pont also discussed plans for the installation of the Phyfe Room: "If I do this of course I would get old door trim, etc; as Charles' [Cornelius], though very attractive, have always annoyed me because they are modern." Yet in the China Hall to the south of the Chinese Parlor, modern details were a necessity. As designed by Thomas Waterman they were more accurate in detail than Cornelius's work. In October 1937, du Pont wrote to Waterman: "Please give me your expert advice on this whole room, and tell me if you approve of the proportions. Also please draw me up a very simple cornice, dado and chair rail. I think that having this material on hand I should like to use it now, and some day if we find a wonderful room, we can always tear it out and do it over again." Even though he was designing the room rather than installing a period interior, Waterman leaned heavily on precedent and du Pont continually looked for substantiation for his designs. In the same letter he queried the architect: "In regard to the shelves for the Lowestoft, if we still keep painted shelves, do you think it would be better to have them perfectly straight in front with a beveled edge, but much thinner than they are now, or would you leave them as is? It seems to me that it would be a mistake to have these shelves mahogany, inasmuch as it is an open cupboard. I have seen plenty of mahogany shelves enclosed with glass doors, but I do not recollect seeing any in open cupboards, do you?" However, four months later du Pont was suggesting a deviation when his sense of design was violated by Waterman's adherence to period example. "Do I see in the sketch that you have split the egg-shaped dado panel in order to open the hidden door underneath the windows? It is a pity to do this, and is there any other method of getting out without doing this? Could we not swing the whole panel as a whole although it might not be quite as correct and old fashioned?" This dialogue between adaptation and authenticity—between overriding aesthetic individuality and the archeological and correct format du Pont had claimed a decade earlier in his correspondence with Sleeper characterized much of the work of revising the 1902 wing at Winterthur.

Du Pont was, by 1935, in his mid-fifties. Du Pont had the benefit of a dozen years of collecting and numerous fine room installations at Chestertown House and in the recent wing. The military determination that had characterized his youth had by now become firmly ingrained in his character. Furthermore, Winterthur had taken on an identity of its own. It had become a devouring passion consuming his time and resources. It was his creation and he was trying to make it perfect. Those around him encouraged his dedication. Even Waterman, who as a designer and as an architectural historian would probably have preferred to create historically correct modern details rather than rob early structures of their elements, conceded: "Any sacrifice is worthwhile to make Winterthur complete. It is so extraordinarily perfect otherwise, each time I see it I am amazed to think anyone could achieve so flawless a thing."

The sacrifice to which he referred was the demolition of Montmorenci, a house from Warren County, North Carolina. That house provided elements for several of the new rooms as well as the staircase that has become the central motif and most memorable symbol of Winterthur in the fifty years since it was installed. Waterman wrote in September 1935: "I must

*China Hall, 1935, before changes in Chinese Parlor, seen through doorway, prompted revisions to this room*

confess I feel a little sad and guilty when I think of Montmorenci, but the stair hall should be glorious...." The stair hall must surely have been the feature that drew du Pont to the house. A few months earlier he had written with barely concealed excitement to his architect: "There is some woodwork...that I might use in the hall. Please keep this strictly under your hat, however, as I don't want it known to anyone in the world. In fact, during the entire trip I am to be known as 'Mr. Francis.' Do you know the best firm that can saw you plaster cornices, etc., move them and copy them? I shall want the head man of that firm to go with us and tell me if they could be moved, give me an estimate, and also tell me whether the old plaster can really be used or not."

Du Pont's concern with anonymity was based on the number of times prices had been inflated when owners discovered who they were dealing with. On one occasion a few years earlier, the price of the paneling he was attempting to acquire through a local dealer had been suddenly jacked up because of "the appearance...of a large expensive sedan driven by a liveried chauffeur, the car bearing Delaware license plates and the passenger in this car requesting the owner to show him the old house."

Du Pont wanted no such repetition when he negotiated for the purchase of the abandoned North Carolina house with its extraordinary staircase and rich cornices, mantels, and moldings. He wisely brought contractor, architect, and workmen to analyze fully the difficulties of removing these features successfully. The next challenge was not simply to install correctly but to adapt the features to the existing structure of the house. The marble staircase of the 1902 wing at Winterthur wrapped

*Chinese Parlor (opposite), July 1935, with the English mantel that was removed after 1937 when an American one was acquired. Montmorenci Stair Hall (above), June 1938. Woodwork from Montmorenci, c. 1822, Shocco Springs, near Warrenton, North Carolina*

around a grand hall of imposing proportions. That hall had of course been the entry for the house but that function had been replaced by the Port Royal entrance in the center of the southern wing. The old front door and porte-cochère had been replaced by a conservatory and the approach to the old stair hall now came from the opposite side of the hall. The grand staircase thus formed the terminus of a prolonged passage through the major entertaining rooms of the wing. It was approached from the side rather than frontally as it had been at Montmorenci. Furthermore, the hall at Winterthur was larger than the hall in North Carolina. Months of discussion among du Pont, Waterman, Benkard, and various contractors resulted in the reworking of the staircase to fit its new function and location. The curve was altered from a circular to an elliptical plan but only after period precedents were discovered. New treads were fabricated out of the monumental wooden columns that once supported the front porch at Montmorenci after it was determined that they were the correct yellow pine. Steel support rods and risers were forced by New Castle County building code. The stairs themselves, fabricated by the Wilmington Stair Co., were widened and the first floor run lengthened to adjust to the height of the space. This brought the visitor to a landing dominated by a graceful Palladian window also removed from the house. The railings at the base of the stairs were opened outward to embrace the visitor effectively as he approached from the lateral entry. Thus the Montmorenci Stair Hall, like the adjoining Red Room and Chinese Parlor, was a modern improvisation incorporating historical woodwork but adjusting to the dimensions of the mansion's stateliest spaces. Other details removed from the house were in-

China Hall (opposite), June 1938, as redesigned by Thomas T. Waterman. The room was created to exhibit a part of George Washington's set of Chinese export porcelain, ordered in 1785 and decorated with the arms of the Society of the Cincinnati. The carving on the side chair and window seat are attributed to Samuel McIntire of Salem, Massachusetts. This chairback settee (above) is part of a group including two chairs (not shown) and a worktable attributed to the shop of John and Thomas Seymour, who worked in Boston from about 1794 to 1804. These carved mahogany and birch inlaid pieces are upholstered with French green silk, or droguet, woven with a fruit and leaf pattern

The exotic patterns on the polychrome delft vase (above) suggest a source for the decoration on English and American seventeenth-century furniture. Traditional motifs were updated with new design ideas transported through smaller objects and through engraved designs in books. The flat stylized carving on the box is typical of New England work, but the inlaid decoration on the Hewlett family kas is a unique surviving example of such work in seventeenth-century America. The Dutch influence is evident in the Hardenbergh Parlor (opposite), and the relationship of various ceramic decorations is shown by the tin-glazed earthenware, salt-glazed stoneware, and oriental porcelains installed here

corporated in the Nemours Room and Library Cross Hall, establishing much of the elegant character of these areas. The same trial and error method that characterized the continuing work in the garden was employed in these improvements. Doorways were set up temporarily and preliminary schemes drawn up by Waterman.

Just as work on the staircase began in earnest, du Pont set out on a world tour. Once again he turned to Bertha Benkard to supervise the final implementation. "In case I should pass out on my world-cruise," he wrote in December of 1935, "I shall appreciate it very much if you will keep on looking after the improvements to the house to their full completion, even to the ornaments which you can move around to your heart's desire. Ruth will know about it and I know she will be only too glad to have you do this for her; but try to get it done before she gets back if possible. I really feel that I can pass away comfortably knowing that the marble stairs will not be left as my memorial."

But it was Waterman who would increasingly control developments at Winterthur, imposing academic ideas on the period installations. Although he wrote a complimentary notice as the staircase neared completion, stating "I think that your taste is fully vindicated," in later installations he pushed for stricter adherence to period example. Wherever possible he lobbied for exact reincorporation of historic woodwork. Two years after the completion of the staircase, du Pont acquired important early woodwork from Morattico, a 1715 house in Richmond County, Virginia, supplementing several scenic panels he already owned from the house. After long discussions, he bowed to Waterman not only in the plan

of the room but in its location at Winterthur. Du Pont had wanted to replace the French parlor between the Chinese Parlor and the Red Room with the Morattico woodwork, but Waterman preferred the billiard room at the eastern end of the 1902 wing. Here the shape, size, and fenestration more closely approximated the period interior. Having accepted Waterman's plan, he later conceded to his sister that the rooms from Morattico are "just as practical for living purposes as before, and greatly improved from a museum point of view." Having agreed with Waterman, he had written to Benkard describing the Billiard Room: "The Morattico Room on the fourth floor is going to be very handsome. It is 13′6″ wide by 23′ long; and the big fireplace with the paintings above it, and the flock paper, will be a wonderful setting for my more or less southern William and Mary furniture. The big gateleg Southampton table is southern. I really think the room is going to be a knock out."

The number of period rooms at Winterthur now far exceeded those for domestic function, and references to their museum function became increasingly common. The interpretation of the collection influenced further acquisitions and took on major importance beside aesthetic considerations. The period and quality of the woodwork in a room also influenced the furnishing decisions. In one example, the Wentworth Room, there was visible evidence of two distinct periods. In response, du Pont wrote, "I still feel that the Wentworth Room is better with the two periods of furniture, the few early oak pieces which could have been put in there when the house was built, and the later pieces of furniture when they put in the fireplace end of the room. I think it is appropriate and logical."

By the early 1940's the economic situation had gradually improved for du Pont, and he was able to continue acquiring important pieces and make the necessary refinements in his collection to accomplish what had become his obvious goal. His letters, however, are full of statements of concern about the fate of the free enterprise system under Roosevelt's administration and fear that people might not continue to enjoy the privileges of wealth. Great houses seemed to him a disappearing feature of the American scene, and he felt that future generations of urban Americans would no longer understand the meaning of country life or the pleasures of a country place. Winterthur was an environment worth preserving for the pleasure and enlightenment of future generations. One of his two daughters was already married and living away from Winterthur, and the other showed no special fondness for the place and the lifestyle it proffered. From every point of view the decision to convert the house totally to a museum seemed logical and inevitable.

By the end of the decade he had successfully reworked the major rooms of the 1902 wing and was at work on minor improvements to the upper floors of the house. Servants' rooms, corridors, and connecting halls were getting new arches and doorways. He wrote to Ives in December 1940: "The house will be more or less dismantled, as I am doing my last changes before we all go to the poorhouse." A year later Ives, by then living in Honolulu, witnessed the bombing of Pearl Harbor and du Pont came face to face with the wartime taxations and restrictions that would fix his determination to turn Winterthur into a museum and open it to the public.

Life at Winterthur during the war was very restricted. The greenhouses and farms were largely shut down and many of the workers went into service or war industry. As in the great country houses in England, the residents of Winterthur settled into the central portion of the wing. The newly completed rooms in the 1902 wing were shut down, the furnishings and textiles put into storage.

Trips to Florida were eliminated for several winters and the house at Southampton, because of its oceanside location, was restricted to blackout conditions. Fuel shortages made wide-ranging travel difficult and du Pont jocularly commented that he barely had enough gas to get him to the front gate of Winterthur in his 16-cylinder Cadillac. Frequent references in his letters reveal his belief that life at Winterthur would never be the same after the war.

In 1942, to satisfy the conditions of the nonprofit status enjoyed by the Winterthur Corporation, small portions of the house were opened to the public. In 1943, the director of the National Gallery approached du Pont regarding the bequest of the collection to that museum and he replied that "the collection has already been provided for." As an interesting footnote, David E. Finley, the first director of the National Gallery, presided at the opening of Winterthur in 1951.

Planning for the postwar period was well under way by 1944. In April of that year, Waterman had suggested installing a series of shop fronts in the Badminton Court and by September du Pont asked Waterman to prepare sketches for such an installation in the Bowling Alley. The search for shop fronts began in 1945. By that time much of the house had

been reopened and the confusion of wartime storage had been sorted out. Curtain and rug storage areas were added in 1946 as well as a paint and carpenter's shop. Work on the transformation of the house into a museum had begun in earnest. The service entrance was transformed into a museum entry. Du Pont suggested other changes in a letter to Albert Ives.

> This winter I am going to do a great many violent things. I am kissing the Bowling Alley good-bye and someday I think it can go into the barn connecting with my Golf cage. Where the Bowling Alley is, I am going to make a brick paved street and I have four shop fronts which will be on this street. The two end shops will be shops that you will be able to get into, and the others probably just to look at. Then the old dancing room is to be put back exactly the way it was in Tappahannock....The third window will be in the Red Lion Shop which was made from the Tappahannock Room and also from the little rooms where we had the gramophone, etc., etc., which went with the dancing room.

Du Pont's determination on this course had been building for a decade, but it was probably reinforced by Bertha Benkard's death in 1945. Perhaps having lost his intimate counsellor, from then on he worked almost exclusively with professional advisers. He leaned heavily on Waterman who, despite failing health, prepared plans for the creation of the shop lane, the reworking of the Dancing and Ping-pong rooms to their original eighteenth-century appearance, and the installation of the glass and Pennsylvania German display areas in portions of the 1902 wing. He also worked on installations on the upper floors previously occupied by servants' rooms. Even the Badminton Court gave way to a series of four facades taken from an inn in Red Lion, Delaware, from Montmorenci, and one mocked up around a Connecticut Valley doorway previously installed at Chestertown House. A fourth facade simulated the appearance of Port

Royal, the Philadelphia house from which so much woodwork for other museum rooms had been obtained. About 1963, it was replaced by the rusticated wood facade of the Banister-MacKaye house from Middletown, Rhode Island.

Du Pont hired his long-time friend and adviser Joseph Downs to prepare a comprehensive and fully illustrated catalogue of the furniture. Downs, along with his assistant, Charles Montgomery, a dealer and pewter specialist from Wallingford, Connecticut, began the arduous task of cataloguing the collection in 1949. It was this team who would form the first professional staff of the museum on its opening in 1951. In the meantime, du Pont began building a home to replace his residence at Winterthur and sited this structure in the shadow of the museum at the foot of the great lawn bordering the bridge that crossed Clenny Run. Here, on the site of a farmhouse cottage that was demolished when its renovation and enlargement proved impractical, he constructed a Regency-style villa and furnished it with the English and French furniture that had been his first collection and had long been used in his New York apartment.

The concentrated energy required must have been enormous. Henry Francis du Pont at seventy-one years could look back on an extraordinary lifetime achievement and express more than a little relief in a letter addressed to Ives on December 28, 1951:

> I still live at Winterthur and my house is called that. The old house is now The Henry Francis du Pont Winterthur Museum, and I am happy to say I don't miss it a bit. It is right there beside me and I naturally can wander around it at will and still get things for it. I have all the fun without the work. Showing people around was getting to be quite exhausting and I am delighted that I have actually seen it finished.

*Shop Lane (opposite), installed in the old bowling alleys, exhibits ceramics and a variety of objects, frequently imported, dating from the mid-eighteenth to the mid-nineteenth century. The shop fronts are from Connecticut, New York State and City, Baltimore, and Alexandria, Virginia, and date from 1800 to 1840. Above left: Charles Willson Peale.* The Accident in Lombard Street, Philadelphia, 1787. *Etching, 8¼ x 11¾". Pitcher (above) from Liverpool, England, 1800–30. Earthenware. Height: 13¼"*

# A MUSEUM FULFILLED

When Winterthur opened to the public in 1951, it was anything but finished. While the opening may have signaled the end of 112 years of occupancy of the house by the du Pont family, it also marked the beginning of a unique and nationally important institution. The foundations of that institution were laid during the last twenty years of private occupancy, during which the house had undergone a complete transformation from a private residence. By 1951, Winterthur had become the home of "the largest and richest assemblage of American decorative arts ever brought together," according to Joseph Downs who, as the former curator of the American Wing at the Metropolitan Museum of Art, was in an ideal position to speak with authority. Yet over the subsequent two decades Winterthur would undergo considerable alteration and expansion largely under the supervision of Henry Francis du Pont. Twenty-five new rooms were added and the collections expanded by nearly five hundred objects a year. Winterthur during these years took on all the requisites of a functioning museum of art.

Although du Pont had hired the team of Joseph Downs and Charles Montgomery to catalogue the collection, it was understood that they were the probable candidates for the first professional jobs at the museum. They were by training and temperament the ideal individuals to forge a viable institution out of a vast private collection. From the beginning of their work at Winterthur they were involved in the physical arrangements made in preparation of the opening. Downs, also a member of the Walpole Society, boasted two decades of museum experience in Philadelphia and New York as well as a personal interest in collecting. He was, logically, du Pont's

*The Lookout was constructed in 1962–63, incorporating a roof designed by Thomas T. Waterman for an earlier structure that was removed during a building expansion. It was positioned on the newly developed Viburnum Hill as a part of the expansion of the gardens undertaken after Winterthur was opened to the public*

201

candidate for the principal curatorial position. Montgomery, on the other hand, had been a dealer with a concentrated interest in pewter but du Pont rightly discerned a talent that would make Montgomery one of the most influential museum professionals in America. In recommending him to the board for the position of executive secretary, du Pont identified important characteristics in Montgomery: "He is hard-headed, capable and an indefatigable worker," he remarked, noting also "his intense enthusiasm for antiques and what they mean and have meant in the American way of life." The meaning of antiques in the American way of life became a bench mark for developments at Winterthur over the next decades as du Pont and the museum's staff sought to refine the collections and their interpretation and to advance scholarship and professionalism in the American decorative arts field.

Du Pont's own interests continued to center on the new rooms at Winterthur and on enlarging the gardens to extend the blooming seasons for visitors who came to Winterthur at times during which the family had traditionally been absent. The Peony Garden, the viburnum plantation, the development of the quarry area with oriental candelabra primulas, and late-blooming azaleas on the slopes adjacent to the quarry and Oak Hill all date from this later period of garden development. Although he had long resisted formal gardens in favor of natural plantations, du Pont, with the assistance of Marian Coffin, created a sundial garden to replace the tennis courts below the Pinetum. As walks and drives were laid out after the visitors' pavilion was constructed in 1961, du Pont found new occasions for landscape activity. Between 1960 and his death nine years

later he had 2,367 species brought to Winterthur. Living now outside the museum, he characterized himself as Winterthur's head gardener, and he took pleasure in visitors' enjoyment of the garden. On his typical early morning tours he charted routes for visitors to follow in order to best see the blooming sequences.

He took a similar interest in the later planning of new museum installations. With his move from the house, many more rooms and service areas had been vacated and were appropriated for museum offices and for exhibition purposes. Du Pont was adamant that all the collections should be on view. Still favoring room settings to gallery display areas, he added new period rooms where he could and also increased the numbers of objects in existing rooms. One by one, the dressing rooms and baths were replaced with display alcoves often amplifying the period of stylistic relationships seen in adjoining rooms. These spaces and major new rooms were all carefully planned with full-scale mock-ups of paneling and furnishings arranged outside the museum before installation. Du Pont described the process in a letter to Ives in June 1948: "I have sold the village of Montchanin to the Wilmington Stair Shop and have started a storage house near the Pike about one-fourth mile above the lodge. It is in a hollow so won't look too big. On the second floor which will eventually be apartments I am going to build exact replicas of the little rooms which will be in the house when it becomes a museum—rooms which are now halls, closets, and bathrooms. I will paint, furnish and curtain these rooms exactly as they will look in the house, so my trustees will know exactly what to do with the alterations." Thus, although he hoped the collections would pro-

*Shaker Dwelling Room (opposite). Woodwork from a stone building, c. 1840, Shaker Community at Enfield, New Hampshire. Paneling in the Gidley Room (above), woodwork from John Gidley house, Newport, Rhode Island, c. 1726*

vide the foundations for the study of American culture, he also wanted the house to reflect his design ideas as well as his previous occupancy. Existing rooms were to be documented and kept intact. He had for a long time kept inventories of rooms including lists of textiles and rugs and the many variations according to seasonal changes and occupancy patterns. He had had Leslie P. Potts, the estate superintendent of Winterthur Farms, draw accurate plans of the location of furniture in each room and now had small markers hammered into the floor to indelibly record furniture locations. One is reminded of his concern of twenty years earlier that the now disassembled Chestertown House be kept just as he occupied it, and in his notes to the Winterthur trustees he even recommended changing dinner table settings every few days to give the spark of life to the house. As in the Chestertown House plan, visitors to Winterthur were to go through the house in groups of four people escorted by a knowledgeable but undemonstrative guide. At Winterthur, tours were scheduled to cover approximately half the house in the morning and the other half in the afternoon with a lunch served in a period room overseen by du Pont's butler. Even with the addition of separate half-day tours, the maximum number of people who could see the museum was sixty. The demand for reservations was overwhelming. Within a few months the museum was booked for a year and a half. In 1952, a garden tour was established during the prime blooming season and a select group of rooms was shown without reservation. Winterthur, one of the best kept secrets in America, had become public.

It required 275 volunteer guides to staff the museum during the first garden tour. Visitors had, in fact, been coming to the fabled gardens for some time, and du Pont had had a preview of what life would be like living in the midst of a popular attraction as early as 1948 when he wrote to Ives: "For two months we have had countless people staying with us—some to see the house and some to see the Azaleas, which were really superb this year. They started blooming early in April and the late ones lasted til almost the end of May. About a thousand people from the Pennsylvania Horticultural Society motored from around Philadelphia to see them one day. Then five hundred people came in special cars from the New York Botanical Garden, and there have been countless small garden clubs, horticulturists, other Azalea growers, etc."

By 1957, the museum was planning a major expansion to accommodate the growing staff and the increased demand from casual visitors and school groups. A new wing was begun to the south of the old service wing incorporating a library and lecture hall, photographic studios, exhibition spaces, and a new visitors' entrance. A capsule survey of American furniture was also included in a dozen or so new period rooms arranged chronologically and thematically to review ideas about the cultural meanings of American domestic artifacts as they had evolved from the study of the Winterthur collections. In addition to the rooms dating from the late seventeenth to the mid-nineteenth century installed in the new South Wing (now called the Washington Wing), thematic displays exploring the influence of commerce, trade, and craftsmanship in colonial America were created. These displays showed the influence of America's relationship to England and the impact of broad restrictions on trade and manufacture. The rise of native craftsmen and the role of technology were graphically demonstrated by the installation of two craftsmen's shops, which represented a virtually unique survival. These shops, which had been actively used by three generations of the Dominy family who worked between 1757 and 1864 in East Hampton, Long Island, contained the tools and templates of three generations of cabinet- and clockmakers. Their primitive tools stood out in remarkable contrast to the finished products and those products of the craft community seen elsewhere in the museum.

Winterthur's emphasis on craft and culture and its interpretation represented as radical a break with tradition as the spirit that prompted du Pont to collect American decorative arts in the face of traditional allegiance to French and English antiques. Despite his own aesthetic predilections and emotional response to antiques, du Pont supported the academic and interpretive bias of the museum staff. From its beginnings, Winterthur was a research and teaching museum. In a way, that notion had its origins in the first published catalogue. In 1952, Joseph Downs's seminal study, the first of three intended volumes covering the furniture collection, was published. With the appearance of *American Furniture: Queen Anne and Chippendale Periods*, a new era of American decorative arts scholarship had begun. In his introduction to the catalogue, du Pont reviewed his own involvement and achievement and pointed a direction for the future:

> During the years that I have collected, I have had many satisfactions and only one regret. The latter is for the things I might have

acquired, but allowed to escape me. My satisfactions are in the contacts I have made with a great number of interesting people, in my greater consciousness of the development of our country, and in my immensely increased appreciation of the generations that have preceded us.

Looking back on it now, I also am glad that I have been able to preserve in some degree the evidences of early life in America, and I am gratified to feel that others too may find my collection a source of knowledge and inspiration.

The new generation was probably best represented by Charles F. Montgomery, who inherited the mantle of leadership at Winterthur on Joseph Downs's death in 1954. Montgomery continued the catalogue process begun by Downs and in 1966 published *American Furniture: The Federal Period 1788–1825*. But Montgomery made his mark on Winterthur not so much as an author or as a curator, but as a teacher. A highly magnetic and influential man, Montgomery possessed the vision of a dreamer and the necessary cunning and skill to achieve his goals. His energy and enthusiasm, wide-ranging interests and concentrated dedication found practical application in new and innovative programs. If du Pont ever came to regret the hardheadedness he had admired it was only because he found in Montgomery a similarly committed and intractable personality. Montgomery continued to make demands on Winterthur's benefactor, stretching the museum's range of activities and with each new idea broadening the dimensions of American decorative arts scholarship and interpretation. Within a year of the museum's opening, he had suc-

cessfully lobbied for the creation of a graduate program in American arts and cultural history at Winterthur in association with the University of Delaware. That program, still the most important arena for graduate study in American decorative arts, is now supplemented by a Ph.D. program. The Winterthur Program has provided professional staff for the museum during its history as well as professional staffs for nearly every major American decorative arts collection in the country.

Montgomery also began lecture programs, annual seminars on museum operation and connoisseurship, and encouraged staff travel and research. He realized that research meant libraries and from the outset planned facilities that under the continued guidance of Frank H. Sommer have become a resource of a quality and complexity comparable to the museum itself. The library collections include both primary and secondary sources on art, architecture, and craft, and on the important corollary areas of history, economics, and sociology. Since 1969, the library has been housed in a research building named in honor of du Pont's sister, Louise Crowninshield, and has expanded rapidly toward filling the copious dimensions of this structure. There are works covering all aspects of American and related European craft, conservation, museum work and historic sites operation, and local and regional history. The rare book hold-

*Piano (opposite) from New York City, 1804–14. John Geib & Son. Mahogany, mahogany veneers, satinwood, brass stringing. Height: 69½". Above: John Trumbull. Washington at Verplanck's Point, New York, 1782. Reviewing the French Troops after the Victory at Yorktown. Inscribed "J. Trumbull, 1790." Oil on canvas, 30 x 20⅛"*

207

ings are models of imaginative acquisition reflecting Sommer's catholic scholarly background and training in archeology and anthropology. European sources of American design, especially architectural design books and theoretical tracts, are a feature of the collection which also includes trade catalogues and craftsmen's price books. Supplementing the published holdings are superb manuscript and archival collections that illuminate the history of craft in America. There are also a separate important manuscript collection assembled by two pioneering scholars of the Shakers, Faith and Edward Deming Andrews, and the research papers of Waldron Phoenix Belknap, Jr., covering early American painting and its relationship to Europe.

Of equal importance to the written record is the visual documentation. Winterthur's own collection is extensively photographed and catalogued. In addition, the library contains a wealth of visual archives providing important corollary information on art, architecture, and decorative arts. In the latter group are ten thousand images assembled by the English furniture scholar R. W. Symonds as well as Winterthur's own assemblage of nearly 126,000 photographs, all forming the Decorative Arts Photographic Collection. This archive includes overall and detail photographs and records of makers marks.

The effort to identify regional origins or to attribute objects to a specific maker or shop tradition is a major area of investigation for the scholar, and other research facilities at Winterthur extend this investigative process beyond the dimensions of documentary research. Regional or national differences in the use of woods for primary and secondary structural elements of furniture was recognized and passed on in an oral tradition in the trade and had little systematic basis. Among the earliest and most important advances made at Winterthur was the scientific analysis of wood specimens. Here again, Charles Montgomery led the way, establishing an organized approach to the recording of wood analysis that now provides an important data base for sorting the maze of misattributions. The scientific approach to decorative arts study was greatly enhanced by the conservation facilities incorporated into the Crowninshield Building that now shelters a variety of research programs. A scientific advisory panel has helped plan the practical application of new technology centering not only on the Winterthur collections but also on the field in general. The systematic analysis of alloy content in metal objects has been especially important in determining the age of forged and cast objects.

Finally, in 1974, a graduate program in the Conservation of Artistic and Historic Objects was founded and like its sister program in American culture produces highly skilled graduates.

The continuing research at Winterthur on American decorative arts in general is disseminated from the museum through an important publishing program which has been responsible for major books including studies of furniture, textiles, metalwork, and craft techniques. The new biennial Winterthur Conference that grew out of Montgomery's symposiums on museum operation and connoisseurship is recorded in a series of published conference proceedings covering such diverse topics as American prints, country cabinetcraft, technological innovation in decorative arts, folk art, and material culture. *Winterthur Portfolio,* published in its

When Oliver Phelps decided to redecorate his house in Suffield, Connecticut, six years after its purchase in 1788, he installed new woodwork and plaster composition ornament in the English style. He papered the parlor with a French block-print wallpaper in a fanciful Etruscan pattern. The linear arabesques, tendril vines, and drapery swags were derived ultimately from the Pompeian frescoes discovered several decades earlier. The Connecticut furniture with which the room is largely furnished shows the simplifications and eccentricities of work from that region, made all the more prominent by contrast with the modish wallpaper. The Federal Parlor is typical of the rooms installed after the museum was opened to the public in 1951

The Hampton Room, from a house built in Elizabeth, New Jersey, in 1761, is furnished with New York pieces. The heavy proportions of overscaled architectural details contrast with the more urbane use of such motifs in Blackwell and Port Royal. The full curves and low-slung proportions of New York furniture amplify the gusto of the woodwork. Reflecting the period practice of covering all furniture with the same textile, much of the furniture and window hangings are made of resist-dyed blue fabric. The silk damask on the easy chair at the right complements the resist, as do the English blue-and-white ceramics, including Worcester and Caughley, which fill the cupboards at either side of the fireplace

Newport, Rhode Island, had close trade ties with
New York and a significant mercantile economy
before the revolution. Waves of influence seemed to
have spread from the prosperous Rhode Island
port into New York and neighboring Connecticut.
A restrained elegance fostered in part by the
innovative designs and fine cabinetwork of the
Townsend and Goddard families gives Newport
furniture a special position in American furniture history. Installed in the Newport Room (left
and above), the shell-carved, block-front desk and
bookcase, attributed to Daniel Goddard, and the
tallcase clock, whose case is attributed to John
Townsend, are perfect expressions of the dignified
reserve of the best Newport work

Pennsylvania was a haven to a variety of religious sects. While the Quakers adapted to city life in Philadelphia and profited from the port economy, the Pennsylvania Germans, clinging to their native language and austere religious principles, peopled the fertile farmlands to the west, forming a separatist community. A Pennsylvania German farmstead yielded a bakehouse, kitchen, and parlor with a rare molded plasterwork ceiling. The Kershner Parlor (above) replaced the Pine Kitchen, a cozy room redolent of the early twen-

tieth-century notion of the colonial interior. By contrast, the bare floors, deep-set curtainless windows, and sparse furnishings are an accurate reflection of Pennsylvania German practice as revealed through period inventories. The furniture follows German precedent but shows the stylistic influence of Philadelphia. The tall inlaid clock was made by Jacob Graff of Lebanon, Pennsylvania. Elsewhere in the room, a shonk (the traditional storage cabinet), a bed, and a five-plate stove indicate the multiple uses of such rooms

Leisure activities were an important part of colonial life. Surviving card tables from the mid-eighteenth century and onward attest to the popularity of board games and such games of skill and chance as backgammon and cards. Fishing poles, battledore rackets, shuttlecocks, and hunting arms recall the role of sport in the colonies. The earliest existing American billiard table (c. 1790-1800) is a masterwork of craftsmanship attributed to John Shaw of Annapolis, Maryland. Shaw also made the sofa seen beneath the portrait of the fabled republican beauty, Mrs. Perez Morton, by Gilbert Stuart. The billiard table came from Wye House, whose later eighteenth-century owner, Edward Lloyd, and family are recorded in Charles Willson Peale's ambitious portrait in the Marlboro Room

213

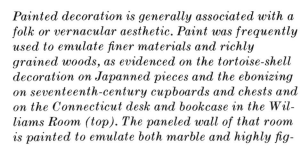

Painted decoration is generally associated with a folk or vernacular aesthetic. Paint was frequently used to emulate finer materials and richly grained woods, as evidenced on the tortoise-shell decoration on Japanned pieces and the ebonizing on seventeenth-century cupboards and chests and on the Connecticut desk and bookcase in the Williams Room (top). The paneled wall of that room is painted to emulate both marble and highly fig-

ured woods. A more abstract approach to painted woodwork is found in the Fraktur Room (above right), with its strong blue pigment and mottled patterns that provide a perfect backdrop for part of the museum's collection of intricately painted religious documents and valentines of the Pennsylvania Germans. The two-story stair hall (above left) that was moved virtually intact from the Ezra Carroll house of c. 1820 in East Springfield, New York, was embellished by itinerant artist William Price with exotic and whimsical scenes recalling the designs of French wallpaper

214

Although the concentration of oriental carpets at Winterthur is an anomaly in relation to period practice, the textile collections present a fair sampling of the important role of fabrics in the home. During the course of the eighteenth century, prosperity made the importation of finer stuffs possible, and the production of domestic goods slowly moved from the individual to professional weavers. In rural villages, domestically produced textiles became tender in the barter system with the local village store, and women of leisure turned their skills toward the production of fancy needlework and stitched embellishments. It is not surprising that much energy of the early industrial revolution was centered in textile produc-

tion. Bed rugs, actively produced from the 1730's to the 1830's, represent a vernacular tradition of home production. Like hooked rugs, these elaborately patterned and brightly colored works have a special appeal to Americana enthusiasts. The bed rug in the Wynkoop Room (above) is hand stitched in loops with a needle and is dated 1748. By contrast, the textiles, wallcoverings, and carpet in the Georgia Dining Room (overleaf), the last period room added to Winterthur, are factory products. The rooms speak of the cosmopolitan prosperity attained in America within fifty years of independence, and the labeled Lannuier dining table is set appropriately with part of the dessert service made in France for President James Monroe

first thirteen volumes as a hardbound annual, has since 1979 been issued quarterly by the University of Chicago Press.

That is a broad spectrum to have grown out of a few halting purchases of American furniture inspired by a glimpse of pink Staffordshire in a pine cupboard in 1923. In fact, the whole enterprise at Winterthur has grown out of a love of and a deep-seated commitment to American objects. The collections are the root of the enterprise and those collections have continued to grow through the dedicated work of the curatorial staff and through the interest of many donors who have understood the importance of the work at Winterthur. The museum's growth and change have reflected new knowledge and discoveries in both history and decorative arts. Gaps in the collection have been filled and study collections added. The textile and print collection and the Ineson-Bissell collection of small silver objects, which serves as an index to makers marks, are important resources which supplement the objects on view. The fakes and forgeries collection provides a touchstone for analysis and an important reminder of the necessity for continuing research and analysis. This collection also provides the gratifying evidence that given the state of knowledge and the already long history of deception in American antiques when du Pont started collecting, he made relatively few mistakes.

Gifts have been a major source of new additions. The paintings collections greatly benefited from Mrs. T. Charlton Henry's gift of an important pair of ancestral portraits by Charles Willson Peale of the colonial physician Benjamin Rush and his wife. In 1959, H. Rodney Sharp presented the William Corbit house (now the Corbit-Sharp House), a 1772 brick Georgian structure twenty-eight miles from Winterthur in the small town of Odessa, Delaware. The Corbit house provides a keen picture of life among the small town squirearchy in the eighteenth century. Since that time other properties in the town have been given to the museum, providing an on-site corollary to the period rooms in the museum. An alternative vision is given by another Winterthur house in Odessa, the David Wilson (now Wilson-Warner) House. This 1769 building and stable (1791) add a special dimension to Winterthur's presentation of craft practices in America. The Brick Hotel (c. 1822), given by Sharp in 1966, and the Collins-Sharp House (c. 1740), given by his sons, complete the suite of Odessa properties now administered by Winterthur.

Gifts have come to the museum in every area of its collections including the library, considerably enhanced over the years through the support of the Friends of Winterthur. Perhaps the most touching gift was made by the children of Mrs. J. Watson Webb, founder of the important collection at Shelburne, Vermont. After her death, Henry Francis du Pont was given the pine dresser, its shelves bulging with the pink Staffordshire which had set him on his collecting path nearly a half-century earlier.

Henry Francis du Pont had labored to bring Winterthur to a certain level of completion during his long lifetime. When it became a museum he continued to support its development, funding the necessary improvements and additions. Not only did he pay for the Crowninshield Research Building and the garden pavilion and visitors' center with its adjoining lecture hall, but he also agreed to fund the air conditioning of the entire building. When it became clear in the late 1950's that a building

that had been pieced together over one hundred years in the humid climate of Delaware was not the ideal environment for the preservation of the collections, Winterthur began a six-year project involving the disassembling of its many rooms to install the necessary duct work. With great logistical skill, the entire project was carried out while the museum was kept open to the public. After this monumental task was accomplished, du Pont may well have thought that Winterthur was truly about to be finished as he approved a major alteration shortly before his death in 1969. He agreed to install a room from Georgia in the old kitchen, the last remaining significant undesignated space, thus completing the representation of rooms from all thirteen original colonies. But he probably knew that no collection ends. As a collector, gardener, and an individual he always looked to the future and new, undreamed-of possibilities. As a builder of a museum he wanted to create a living institution serving present need but with the ability to change and adapt. He passed on his commitment to excellence and a clear-eyed view of the future. That was an ideal inheritance for the custodians of the Winterthur patrimony.

Henry Francis du Pont was, in effect, the first director of the Winterthur Museum. In the years since its public opening, a series of highly esteemed professionals have assumed the helm and pushed the museum inevitably forward. Edgar P. Richardson, a distinguished scholar of American painting and the director of the Detroit Institute of Arts, succeeded Charles F. Montgomery. He added significantly to the paintings collection, filling the most serious gap in du Pont's collecting strategy. He was succeeded by Charles van Ravenswaay, formerly of the regional his-

tory museum at Old Sturbridge Village in Massachusetts. Van Raven-swaay brought the skills of a historic sites manager to Winterthur and carried the museum through the transition period after Henry Francis du Pont's death. His successor, James Morton Smith, the director of the State Historical Society of Wisconsin, brought an energetic midwestern populism to Winterthur, enlarging the museum's audience through expanded tours and increased availability of the gardens. The current director, Thomas A. Graves, Jr., formerly the president of the College of William and Mary, confirms the commitment to high levels of academic achievement that have always distinguished Winterthur. That special quality and the museum's national significance have been repeatedly evidenced through the numerous sustaining foundation grants the museum has received.

The traditional tasks of a museum to preserve, record, display, and interpret have all evolved at Winterthur and in fact have set standards for emulation. The peculiar nature of Winterthur, the fact that there is, indeed "nothing of a museum in the air," that the collections are injected with a lively intimacy, is attributable to the continuation of the display techniques inaugurated by du Pont. Seasonal changes still reflect the influence of nature on life and mirror the proximity of the gardens to the house. Flowers in the rooms are a reminder of seasons past and present and seasonal changes are further indicated by specialized displays and tours. Although the farms are closed and the herds dispersed, Winterthur still maintains the feeling of a country place. A museum in motion, it is also, as its founder wished, a place of rest and reflection. Du Pont had writ-

*Pier table (opposite) from Philadelphia, c. 1825–40. Mahogany veneers, cherry, tulip, pine, gilt, and verde antique decoration. Height: 43⅞". Above: Nicolino V. Calyo. Harlem, The Estate of Dr. Edmondson, near Baltimore, Maryland, 1834. Gouache on paper, 16¾ x 29⅞"*

219

ten: "I sincerely hope that the Museum will be a continuing source of inspiration and education for all time, and that the gardens and grounds will themselves be a country place museum where visitors may enjoy as I have, not only the flowers, trees, and shrubs, but also the sunlit meadows, shady wood paths, and the peace and quiet calm of a country place which has been loved and taken care of for three generations."

The giant oaks and poplars still crown the hillsides and shade the lawns. Newly tenanted fields remind the visitor of the thriving activity that once animated the landscape. Winterthur is now encircled by country club, retirement home, and other protected enterprises that will preserve its boundaries and its rural demeanor. In the increasingly urban Atlantic corridor, Winterthur is a place apart. It is a world of dreams, not in the sense of fantasy, but in the best definition of dreams as ideals and aspirations capable of fulfillment. Winterthur, like the industrial growth that spawned it, is a great American enterprise and a national resource. Over the years its identity will change but its collections, their presentation, and interpretation are the foundations of its personality and the keys to its future.

Some years ago Henry Francis du Pont was busy overseeing the installation of one of the new rooms in the museum. As deeply involved in the project as he had been in his first room a half-century earlier, he threw himself into the work. When it was arranged to his satisfaction he turned to leave but took a quick glance backward and paused appreciatively, saying, "It's a pretty swell room. As a matter of fact, it's a pretty swell museum—the Winterthur Museum." He was right!

*Charleston Dining Room (above). Woodwork from William Burrows house, c. 1772, Charleston, South Carolina. Presentation medal (opposite) from New York, 1832. Made by Marquand Brothers, designed by Thomas Brown. Gold. Height: 4⅝". Presented to the Marquis de Lafayette by the 27th New York State Artillery*

# AFTERWORD

H orace Walpole, son of Robert Walpole, one of eighteenth-century England's most powerful politicians, chose to establish his identity in a different arena from that of his father. In 1749, at thirty-two, the young Walpole purchased a country estate in Twickenham, a two-hour coach ride from London along the road to Hampton Court. The house, Strawberry Hill, sat on a gentle slope overlooking the Thames. Walpole, who had rented the "cottage" for two years prior to its purchase, immediately began laying plans for reworking the house to suit his taste.

Only a few close friends were aware that Horace Walpole's taste in interior decoration was Gothic! The Gothic style, to most knowledgeable Englishmen, was an old-fashioned ecclesiastical style, hardly appropriate for the country home of a proper English gentleman. Walpole, however, deliberately chose an "underdog" style whose freedom of lines appealed to the maverick streak in him. The Gothic, as he saw it, was free from "the tyranny of rule" in a way the classical style could never be. It was also a "patriotic" style, faithful to medieval and early modern English traditions. Walpole and his antiquarian friends spent long hours poring over old engravings of churches and tombs and in working up plans for transposing ecclesiastical ornamentation into domestic settings. For forty years Walpole reworked Strawberry Hill, creating an eighteenth-century museum of Gothic ornament in domestic scale that offered to his many visitors a disarming mixture of "elegance and surprise." As the popularity of Strawberry Hill grew, sparking a revival of interest in the Gothic taste, Walpole issued reserved tickets of admission to four people a day between

*Sampler. American, 1794. Made by Susan Smith. Silk embroidery on canvas, 16¾ x 16¾"*

223

the hours of 12:00 noon and 3:00 p.m. from May through September.

Horace Walpole's reputation as the restorer of the Gothic style was matched by his fame as a collector and a chronicler of his times. Just as fervently as he built Strawberry Hill for over forty years, he collected. A full catalogue of the collection was printed by Walpole in 1784, and at his death Walpole left copies to eighty of his best friends. The sale of his collection in 1842 took thirty-two days!

In the catalogue of his "villa," printed on a private press at Strawberry Hill and compiled primarily to assist visitors, the spirit of Walpole's achievements permeates the detailed room descriptions.

> The Great North Bedchamber is hung with crimson Norwich damask. The bed is of tapestry of Aubusson, festoons of flowers on a white ground, lined with crimson silk, plumes of ostrich feathers at the corners. Six elbow chairs of the same tapestry, with white and gold frames; and six ebony chairs. A carpet of the manufacture of Moorfields; a foot-carpet of needle-work; and a firescreen of the tapestry of the Gobelins.
>
> The chimney was designed by Mr. Walpole from the tomb of W. Dudley, bishop of Durham, in Westminster-abbey, and is of Portland stone, gilt; with dogs of ormoulu with arms and trophies; the chimney-back is ancient, and bears the arms of Henry 7th. On the hearth, two old red china bottles.
>
> Over the chimney, a large picture of Henry 8th, and his children; bought out of the collection of James West, esq. in 1773....

The list for the Great North Bedchamber continues for seven more pages. As an eighteenth-century ballad summed up the reputation of Walpole's home:

> Some cry up Gunnersbury,
>     For Sion some declare;
> And some say that with Chiswick-house
>     No villa can compare;
> But ask the beaux of Middlesex,
>     Who know the country well,
> If Strawb'ry-hill, if Strawb'ry-hill
>     Don't bear away the bell?

As zealously as Walpole built and collected, so he wrote. Walpole self-consciously developed his correspondence with friends in order to provide an alternate record of the events of his lifetime, more truthful, more witty, and more colorful than the record of newspapers and public documents. Much of Walpole's voluminous correspondence has been published by Yale University Press.

Horace Walpole also composed essays on gardening and landscape design. His *History of the Modern Taste in Gardening* passed through numerous editions in the 1780's and 1790's and established Walpole as a leading advocate of a naturalistic landscape movement that preferred "irregularity" (Hogarth's line of beauty) and "inexhaustible diversity" to symmetry. For Walpole, the naturalistic landscape park was an English invention and therefore as "patriotic" as the Gothic style in architecture. Through his own garden experiments at Strawberry Hill, his essays on landscape design, and his letters commenting on prominent gardens throughout England, Walpole exercised a powerful social influence on the spread of the "imitation of nature" in eighteenth-century English gardening.

In the early twentieth century in the United States, an enthusiastic group of collectors turned to Horace Walpole's writings for inspiration and validation. They, too, were interested in an "underdog" taste, although it was not Walpole's Gothic. These gentlemen antiquarians, including private collectors and museum and library professionals, were devotees of American colonial antiques (with colonial loosely defined as the period from settlement to 1840), and promoters of what would come to be called the Colonial Revival. They banded together to learn from one another, to share their enthusiasm, and to promote their interests, especially through publications. Founded in 1910, the Walpole Society quickly became the most prestigious society of collectors of Americana in the world.

Among the Walpole Society membership in its early years, no one was more dedicated than Norman M. Isham, whose *In Praise of Antiquaries* was published by the society in 1931 to great approbation by the membership. A fellow Walpolean described Isham at seventy as a devoted "old house" man who had recently jumped from a moving automobile in his excitement to get a closer look at an outstanding ruin of early architecture. "The enthusiasm of the collector of silver or glass or furniture is equally deep seated, but it seldom finds release in violent physical action," said Lawrence C. Wroth in *The Walpole Society: Five Decades* (1960).

The Walpole Society expanded its publishing activities in the 1920–1940 period by issuing annual *Notebooks* as well as special monographs such as Isham's *Early American Houses* (1928), Alfred C. Prime's posthumous *Arts and Crafts In Philadelphia, Maryland, and South Carolina: Gleanings from Newspapers Collected by Alfred C. Prime* (1929), their own *Twenty-fifth Anniversary of The Walpole Society* (1935), Hollis French's *Jacob Hurd and His Sons Nathaniel and Benjamin* (1939), and John Hill Morgan's *John Singleton Copley* (1939). After 1940 the expense of publishing slowed their activity, but individual members, such as Thomas T. Waterman, continued to publish their work through other outlets.

With the exception of Edwin Atlee Barber and Alfred Coxe Prime of Philadelphia, the Walpole Society up to 1932 was dominated by New Yorkers and New Englanders. In 1932 the society elected Henry Francis du Pont (1880–1969), a relatively new collector who had just completed a major phase of the reworking of his family's country estate at Winterthur, Delaware. Du Pont became an enthusiastic member of the Walpole Society, and in 1948 was one of five Walpoleans to underwrite the costs of publishing a history of the society. In turn, members of the Walpole Society were ecstatic about du Pont's collection, which they saw for the first time in 1932:

> The visit to Mr. du Pont's house, on Saturday, was something unique in Walpole experience. That group of peripatetics has seen many early American rooms in many places.... All kinds have we passed through in museum after museum, but they were all rooms—museum rooms, silent places with polished floors, filled with polished, si-

lent furniture standing in polite but aristocratic aloofness. Study and admiration they invite; intimacy is impossible....Yet never have we seen so many old American rooms under one roof. Nor could we imagine that there could be put into one house so many rooms so different, in size, period and character, in such way as to make it liveable—to make a home of it. But Mr. du Pont has done it. Here are rooms that welcome the guest, furniture which seems glad to receive him. There is nothing of the museum in the air.

Henry Francis du Pont's achievement—Winterthur—far outstrips the contributions to American culture of most of his fellow Walpoleans. Unlike his collector friends, H. F. du Pont had the imagination and resources to create a permanent museum to preserve the glories of American artistry and craftsmanship. He called upon many of his fellow Walpoleans for professional assistance and inspiration, most notably Joseph Downs, Russell Kettell, and Thomas Waterman. H. F. du Pont seems to have had a clear vision of establishing his identity, à la Horace Walpole, by reworking his country house in an "underdog" but "patriotic" American colonial style, and in leaving it, along with its collections and the gardens (in an English-style naturalistic landscape park), as a legacy to the American people.

But H. F. du Pont, like Horace Walpole, was not merely a great collector. The emblem of the Walpole Society is a silver lamp set upon books. The society's goal has always been preservation *and* the promotion of learning. H. F. du Pont upheld this Walpolean ideal with enthusiasm and tenacity, first by calling upon expert help from friends, then by hiring his own experts, and finally by establishing a corporation for perpetuating his goals through programs of professional training and publication. Winterthur opened to the public in 1951. In 1952 the museum joined with the University of Delaware in creating the nation's first graduate program for study in the American decorative arts. Clearly, H. F. du Pont had passed from the private phase of his collecting to an academic and public phase. Although he never relinquished control over his creation, du Pont sought to guarantee its future, and maximize his contribution to American culture, through professionalization.

One of H. F. du Pont's most productive professional relationships was that established with Joseph Downs, a curator of decorative arts elected to the Walpole Society in 1935. Downs had just come to the American Wing of the Metropolitan Museum of Art after a successful stint at the Philadelphia Museum of Art, where he worked with its flamboyant director, Fiske Kimball, in creating American period rooms. By the late 1940's, H. F. du Pont was certain that he wanted his collection published and that Downs was the best person to do it. In 1948 he presented a plan to Downs and Charles F. Montgomery for a room-by-room catalogue of his collection set in a chronological framework. Du Pont envisioned several volumes over a five-year period, after which time Downs was to become Winterthur's first paid curator. Downs accepted the offer and in 1949 left the American Wing for Winterthur.

The room-by-room format desired by H. F. du Pont was eventually set aside to concentrate on a definitive history of American furniture. Joseph Downs published the landmark *American Furniture: Queen*

*Anne and Chippendale Periods, 1725–1788* (1952) before his death in September 1954. His assistant, Charles F. Montgomery, succeeded him as Winterthur's curator. Montgomery soon became the museum's first director and eventually published a second volume, *American Furniture: The Federal Period, 1788–1825* (1966). When Montgomery departed for Yale University in 1970, his research assistant, Benno M. Forman, inherited the mantle. Forman's *American Seating Furniture, 1630–1730*, the third volume in the series, will be published by the Winterthur Museum in 1986.

H. F. du Pont's dream of a room-by-room catalogue, initiated in the 1920s when he was assembling his early collection at Chestertown House on Long Island, was partially fulfilled with the publication of John A. H. Sweeney's *Treasure House of Early American Rooms* in 1963. Until now, Sweeney's book has been the only comprehensive pictorial presentation of Winterthur available to the general public. *Winterthur*, this new and larger book by Jay E. Cantor, fills a long-identified need for a fresh treatment of Winterthur. The spectacular new photography by Lizzie Himmel conveys the elegance and beauty of Winterthur. The text by Cantor, appropriately a graduate of the Winterthur Program in Early American Culture, offers the reader the elements of surprise and delight as one anecdote after another reveals the story of the development of Winterthur. Those same emotions—surprise and delight—were the almost daily reward of collectors such as Horace Walpole and Henry Francis du Pont. Cantor satisfies the craving for detailed explanations of the instincts and habits of a great collector. He sets Winterthur into its social context, offering many insights not only into the creation of Winterthur but also into the development of interest in American decorative arts generally. Together the text and pictures tell the story of Winterthur more fully than any previous publication, and provide a spellbinding chronicle of one man's encounter with the American colonial past. The results of Henry Francis du Pont's obsession are a museum, a garden, and an educational institution of national rank.

Scott T. Swank
Deputy Director for Interpretation
Winterthur Museum and Gardens
February 1985

# ACKNOWLEDGMENTS AND CREDITS

The opportunity to "go home again," to go back to Winterthur, where I was a student twenty years ago and which I first visited as a schoolboy thirty years ago, has been precious and rewarding. Many of the museum staff were my teachers and continued to provide hope and guidance in sorting through the vast collection and the equally extensive documentation surrounding it. John Sweeney, who had dedicated his own research to assembling information about Henry Francis du Pont, shared the results of his years of study with me. Both he and Charles Hummel, Deputy Director, Department for 'Collections, pointed out many details that would otherwise have gone unnoticed. Along with Scott T. Swank, Deputy Director, Department for Interpretation, they read my manuscript and made important suggestions. Ian M.G. Quimby, Head of Publications, not only read the manuscript and coordinated the comments of all the readers but oversaw all aspects of Winterthur's contribution to the production of this volume. He worked closely with Lizzie Himmel in arranging the photography of the rooms, an effort perfectly justified by the exciting color photographs which enliven this book. Quimby also oversaw the preparation of the museum's object photography. His enthusiasm and support made a seemingly impossible task easy. He also secured the support of James Morton Smith, former director of Winterthur, and the continued involvement of Thomas Graves, the present director.

Others at the museum provided invaluable assistance at every turn. Paul Hensley, the archivist; Beatrice Taylor, the manuscript librarian; and Neville Thompson, Librarian, Printed Books and Periodicals; made every research source readily accessible as did Nancy Goyne Evans, Karol Schmiegel, and Marian Blakeman in the Registrar's Office. The curatorial staff willingly accepted a stranger in their midst, and Phillip Curtis, Sue Swan, and Donald Fennimore provided special assistance in their areas of ceramics and glass, textiles, and metalwork. Philip Correll guided me through the gardens and grounds and provided important plant identifications. Alberta Brandt and Alma Sorber were untiring in processing large photograph orders, and the housekeeping staff under the supervision of Everett Boyce did yeoman service in removing the filtering windows to allow the natural light to flood these rooms once more.

Of those who knew Winterthur in the years it was the du Pont home or in its nascence as a museum, Pauline Louise du Pont Harrison, Henry F. du Pont Harrison, Pamela Copeland, Averell du Pont, George Weymouth, Alice Winchester, Ralph

Carpenter, Richard Wunder, Harold Sack, Charlotte Sittig, David Stockwell, E. McClung Fleming, and Florence Montgomery all graciously shared their experiences and insights with me. Special thanks go to my colleagues at Christie's, Debra Force and Jeanne Vibert, who also read my manuscript and helped focus my ideas. Jenny Long and Joanne Klein of my staff helped by coping when work on this volume kept me out of the office (or in a bad mood when I was in it).

Had she not gone into publishing, my editor at Abrams, Joan Fisher, who directed the project, would have made an excellent doctor as she wielded the editor's pen with the sensitivity of a surgeon. I came away from the editing process feeling both intact and improved. We both thank Cecile deLarue for typing the legible parts of my manuscript. Thanks also go to Margaret Rennolds, editorial assistant, for her unflagging attention to the processing of the book.

I can claim only partial credit for the information in this volume. Research about Winterthur's collections has been going on since 1949 when Joseph Downs and Charles Montgomery began the first comprehensive study of the furniture. Since that time curators and registrars, students and visiting scholars, dealers and guides have studied and recorded much about the collections. I have freely drawn on their work.

Among the most dedicated members of the museum family are the several hundred guides who energetically devote themselves to interpreting the collections to visitors. They have enthusiastically pressed me to complete this book so that they and others could learn more of the mysterious origins of what is truly a great work of art. To them, to my parents and all my other teachers, and to my classmates and fellow graduates of the Winterthur Program in Early American Culture, this book is dedicated.

The sections dealing with Henry Francis du Pont's horticultural training and activity come almost entirely from the recent research of garden historian Valencia Libby.

## A Note on Published Sources

The information in this book derives largely from manuscript sources, registrar's files, and personal reminiscences. Several publications about the museum have been invaluable. *The Winterthur Story*, which first appeared in the *Winterthur Portfolio* I, 1964, has important articles about the house and gardens by E. McClung Fleming, Charles F. Montgomery, Jonathan Fairbanks, John A.H. Sweeney, and C. Gordon Tyrrell. John Sweeney's volume *Winterthur Illustrated* (Winterthur, 1963) provides a useful overview of the rooms at the museum. Scott Swank's article "Henry Francis du Pont and Pennsylvania German Folk Art" in *Arts of the Pennsylvania Germans* (New York, W.W. Norton, 1983) was especially useful as were the many guiding manuals and internally generated room studies in Winterthur files.

*The Walpole Society Notebooks*, published annually since 1926, are a major index to collecting patterns, and Elizabeth Stillinger's *The Antiquers* (New York, Alfred Knopf, 1980) is the best modern source on the history of American collecting. Also useful for the chapters on collecting were *Francis P. Garvan, Collector* (New Haven, Yale University Art Gallery, 1980), Henry Watson Kent's *What I Am Pleased to Call My Education* (New York, The Grolier Club, 1949), Charles B. Hosmer, Jr., *Preservation Comes of Age*, 2 volumes (Charlottesville, The University Press of Virginia, 1981), and Neil Harris's *Winterthur and America's Museum Age* (Winterthur Museum, 1981). In addition to Valencia Libby's unpublished thesis, Norman B. Wilkinson's *E.I. du Pont Botaniste* (Charlottesville, The University Press of Virginia, 1972) and Harold Bruce's *Winterthur in Bloom* provided useful information on gardens.                                                                      J.E.C.

## Photograph Credits

All photographs are by Lizzie Himmel except those on the pages listed here. Courtesy Winterthur Museum: 18–24, 27–38, 39, 44–49, 50 (top and bottom right), 51 (top and bottom right), 54 (bottom right), 57, 66, 67 (right), 68, 69, 72–76, 90, 91, 95–101, 114 (bottom), 116, 118–131, 133–160, 178–184, 185 (bottom left), 189–192, 198, 199, 204–207, 218–222. Courtesy Eleutherian Mills Historical Library: 26, 66, 67, 70, 71. Courtesy The Society for The Preservation of New England Antiquities: 114. Courtesy Girl Scouts of the U.S.A.: 93.

# INDEX

230